# Digital in the Boardroom

# Digital in the Boardroom

Jennifer Wolfe

Copyright © 2016 Jennifer Wolfe
All rights reserved.

ISBN-13: 9781519489517
ISBN-10: 151948951X
Library of Congress Control Number: 2015919634
CreateSpace Independent Publishing Platform
North Charleston, South Carolina

# ACKNOWLEDGMENTS

I extend my heartfelt thanks to those who have continually supported me in my career and specifically in the writing of this book: my longtime mentor, friend, and coauthor of *Brand Rewired* and *Domain Names Rewired*, Anne Chasser. My trusted research analysts and support team, Jake Dressman and Samantha Bergman. And to my husband, Wolfie, and son, Jack, thank you for your unconditional love and support as I continue on this journey.

And, to my friends and colleagues who have offered kind words for this book, Diane Strahan, Cynthia Gibson, Denise Kuprionis, and Ryan McKillen, thank you so very much for your incredibly valuable time, feedback, and generosity to me over the years and in providing support for *Digital in the Boardroom*.

# PROLOGUE

*Digital* is one of those buzzwords we've seen thrown around a lot in the last five years. Marketers have come to define it as everything that comes through a device that accesses the Internet. In what have been dubbed "the years of digital transformation," it's likely that digital spending will eclipse traditional marketing in the very near future; online spending is already quickly approaching traditional retail spending. Organizations have struggled to keep up amid accelerating technology growth and rapid adoption by even "old-school" generations. The next generation is composed of preteens and teens who have had smartphones or tablets in their hands since kindergarten and a culture that revolves around texts and social media.

The notion of cyberattack is no longer just a threat or a fear hidden in the information-technology department but is now front and center as the world has watched nefarious actors prey on some of the biggest companies in the world during the holiday shopping season, stealing credit-card information and threatening the very idea of free speech by holding Sony hostage if it released a movie they didn't like.

The traditional roles of C-suite executives—like the chief marketing officer, chief information officer or chief technology officer, and chief legal officer—have had to evolve, and how a CEO and a board oversee these functions is rapidly changing. Digital is no longer just for the Facebooks, Googles, or Amazons of the world but is for every company. Every company functions digitally, and every company will continually evolve in managing digital in the coming years.

Responsibilities are shifting, and in many cases, executives and directors need new tools and skill sets to effectively manage what lies ahead.

I wrote this book as a guide for directors and senior executives to understand how to identify signals of change in the digital world and to be prepared for the changes coming in all facets of digital. It's broken down into the following categories:

1. The signals of change, the next generation of the Internet, and new top-level domains
2. Cybersecurity, search, social networking, mobile, and the "Internet of things" (watches, smart houses, smart cars, smart thermostats—all of the things that now connect to the Internet that didn't before)
3. Content and data optimization
4. The role of digital in the boardroom, including suggestions on how to manage digital at the board level

My team has spent the last four years researching the impact the next generation of the Internet will have on search-engine optimization, how Google will respond, how data will change and what new data could be gathered, how the user experience will change, and how the changing Internet naming system integrates with mobile, the Internet of things, and social media. We also track patents being filed by big technology companies to forecast future trends in digital, continually research industry shifts and the implications of big mergers, and forecast future assumptions about the Internet in working with our global client base. I've compiled years of research across board studies, cybersecurity reports, and headlines in major publications to create this guide to help board members navigate this increasingly complex and rapidly changing digital environment.

I've also seen the struggles some organizations have in battling the status-quo mentality, and when I wrote my previous two books, *Brand Rewired* and *Domain Names Rewired* (which Wiley published in 2010 and

2013, respectively), I interviewed executives from leading global companies like Procter & Gamble, Microsoft, Yahoo!, Harley-Davidson, Kraft Foods, General Mills, Intel, Warner Bros., Kodak, Kimberly-Clark, International Paper, Verizon, Scripps Networks Interactive, Time Warner, and more. From those interviews, I began to understand how silos operate in organizations and what is needed to overcome them and build in more collaborative and open processes to manage digital in the future.

Over the last four years, I've briefed CEOs and CFOs of major corporations on the next generation of the Internet. I've also briefed executives at various levels of organizations and seen the status-quo culture at work, which often impedes senior executives from learning about important changes in the operation of the Internet and thereby missing an important new opportunity.

As I struggled with these issues, I searched for books that addressed the future of digital and how to manage digital in the boardroom. My favorite book about the future of digital is by Google's chairman, Eric Schmidt, and his coauthor, Jared Cohen: *The New Digital Age*, which I reference in this book. If you haven't read it, I highly recommend it. I've studied the reports and white papers put out by the biggest consulting companies in the world on various facets of digital, and I noticed that most of the studies dig deep into specific issues, but few pull all of the pieces together, mirroring the challenge in most organizations (each leader is specialized in a specific area, but few have the horizontal view). So, I've compiled that research as well and assembled it into an easy-to-read guide for senior executives and board members, offering you what you need to know about digital as it is today, how to predict digital trends in the future, and what you may want to consider in managing digital in the future.

As boards become responsible to shareholders for oversight of data management and security and the issue of digital obsolescence becomes a real threat to the future of many companies, *Digital in the Boardroom* is more important than ever before.

I hope you will find that this book shines a light on not just the threats of inaction but also on the opportunities of being proactive in bringing digital into the boardroom, setting the leadership vision and tone to eliminate a status-quo culture and preparing for the future of digital in your company.

Digital in the Boardroom:
The Way We Use the Internet Has Changed—Has Your Company?

# CONTENTS

Acknowledgments .................................... v
Prologue ........................................... vii

Chapter 1  Signals of Change ........................... 1
Chapter 2  The Big Bang no One Heard ................. 34
Chapter 3  The Cybersecurity Threat .................. 59
Chapter 4  Search Rewired ............................ 89
Chapter 5  The Social-Network Revolution:
           when the People Took Over ................ 108
Chapter 6  Mobile, Apps, and the Internet of Things .. 128
Chapter 7  Everything Will Change, but Good
           Content Will Always Be King .............. 143
Chapter 8  Big Data Optimized Is Digital Intelligence .. 154
Chapter 9  Digital in the Boardroom .................. 175

About the Author ................................... 185
Bibliography by Chapter ............................ 187

*Chapter 1*

# SIGNALS OF CHANGE

Fig. 1.1. Associated Press. Reprinted with permission.

Jennifer Wolfe

In 2005, the ascent of Pope Benedict XVI was announced to a crowd of faithful Catholics in Saint Peter's Square. Traditional news media spread the word to the rest of us. Just eight years later, in 2013, the installation of Pope Francis was announced to a crowd of faithful Catholics—and all of their friends, and their friends' friends, and their friends' friends' friends—in a one-to-many celebration via mobile devices and social networking. In the last ten years, the digital signals of change have been all around us. They're easy to see; we experience them every day. But, like much of big data, until you put it together and look for signals and meaning, it's just the photo of

Fig. 1.2 *Wall Street Journal* Headlines from 2012 - 2014

the day. Much like the Associated Press photo shown in 2005 and again in 2013, until you put them next to each other, the meaning isn't clear.

You might read the paper every day, but until you stack up the headlines over a couple of years, you might not see the trends. Take a look at this chronological stack of headlines from the *Wall Street Journal*.

By scanning just a few digital article titles from the last three to four years in the *Wall Street Journal's* coverage of mainstream media, we can see that we are now close to the time when people consume all of their content on the Internet versus cable TV. Twitter is impacting what we see on TV. The Weather Channel is forecasting what we buy. Netflix, Hulu, and other Internet-only venues have the audacity to create their own programming. (While many predicted that Netflix's own production was a long shot, a year later, it was a top Emmy winner. And now, many binge-watch its new programs, an entire season at a time, as soon as they are released.) Traditional publishing is dying and evaluating Netflix-like business models. Facebook, Google, and Amazon are all creating original content. Amazon wants to use drones to offer same-day delivery to our homes, because two-day Prime isn't fast enough. Data is driving research and development and e-commerce in profound new ways. Companies like Target and Home Depot have learned the hard way what a security breach can cost, causing information-technology departments everywhere to reassess the rapidly expanding digital way in which employees in their companies interact with outside vendors and leave them exposed. And in late 2014, the biggest story of all was when Sony was hacked and had some embarrassing e-mails leaked—at that moment, every company realized its true vulnerabilities.

Things are changing rapidly in the digital world, but flash back seventeen years. The Internet became "the next big thing" in 1999 with the explosion of the dot-com business model. Fortunes were made and lost in the dot-com bubble. Cell phones had just started to become affordable to the masses in the late 1990s, but all we could do was talk or e-mail on those early versions of cell phones. Smartphones didn't exist back then.

We didn't have social media, YouTube, or reality-TV stars. And, as for entertainment, we watched our TVs with the channels our cable providers offered. If we wanted to see our favorite shows, we actually had to tune in at the scheduled times to watch, or we'd miss them.

We've come a long way in the last seventeen years. In the last fifteen, our world has been transformed by technology, and social culture has shifted dramatically in a very short time. We actually now live and work in two different worlds: a digital world connected by the Internet and devices, and the real world, where we actually physically show up places to engage in daily life and interact with other live people. That sounds kind of crazy, but so did reality TV when it first started.

When trying to oversee and manage how executives in your company are preparing for the future of your digital world, it's important to notice everything that has already happened and to look for the signals of what will come so that you are prepared and can make smart business investments. Investing in the wrong things leads you to bankruptcy or obsolescence. Investing in the right things will change the world. What will people want and need that they may not even know they want or need yet? Sounds like a simple enough question to answer. That's what Steve Jobs, Mark Zuckerberg, Larry Page and Sergey Brin, and Jeff Bezos all excelled at over the last seventeen years. They amassed billion-dollar fortunes and changed the world with their ideas and their companies.

To really see the future of your business in a digital world, you have to be willing to think in a way that others don't. You have to be willing to sometimes start with a blank canvas and reimagine how people could live and work if all of our assumptions change. In the digital world, we've essentially been modifying the original home page concept and upgrading it every year with new technologies or graphics, maybe new content or messaging. Search-engine experts weigh in annually on the latest ways to generate better organic search results. And as new fads become new realities—like how people live in social networks or how they rely on apps instead of browsers on mobile devices—companies plug those holes. But we've been doing this so rapidly over the last fifteen years that, in many instances, companies haven't stopped to rethink the whole digital world. They just keep plugging holes.

As I state in the prologue, I wrote this book for C-suite executives and directors on private and public company boards to understand the role of digital in the boardroom. According to the 2015 PricewaterhouseCoopers (PwC) Annual Corporate Director's Survey, 46 percent of respondents believed they should spend more time on strategic planning and 54 percent believed they should spend more time on IT (i.e., digital) strategy and cybersecurity. I'll cover many of the drivers of change in how people search and navigate the Internet and examples of how digital shifts have occurred in the past.

In every company's boardroom, leaders must be able to consider and hypothesize about the future for the benefit of shareholders or investors. But to see the future, we have to start by fundamentally understanding how people are living their lives today and identify these signals of change so we can be open to receiving the messages of what could be and what to do in response to them. I've mapped this out in three key steps for digital in the boardroom:

1. Turn off the status-quo mentality, which could lead you to obsolescence.
2. Look at the signals so that you can predict the future of digital and how it impacts your company.
3. Map your digital world and paint the future, ensuring your digital strategy will protect you and take you where your company needs to be.

## STEP ONE: TURN OFF THE STATUS-QUO MENTALITY

One of the biggest roadblocks in organizations when it comes to digital—large or small, entrepreneurial or stalwart blue chip—is the status quo. The status quo is what prevents most organizations from achieving the results they seek. Surprisingly, even some of the most innovative companies develop status-quo mentalities as they grow larger, resulting in poorer performance.

I've seen this firsthand in my consulting work with Fortune 500 companies, evaluating what could be a paradigm shift in the way people use the Internet: new top-level domains (we'll cover these extensively in the next chapter). A top-level domain is what comes after the "dot" in *dot-com* or *dot-org* (or now, *dot-google*). In brief, these new top-level domains create new opportunities for companies to address security, data, and authenticity and to connect all facets of their digital worlds in a new way. My job as an expert on how companies can use branded top-level domains has drawn much conversation from high-level executives who simply say, "People will always want dot-coms," or, "This will fail," or—my favorite—"This is at least ten years away."

When given an opportunity to own its own channel of the Internet and control one of its most important digital assets for the first time in the history of the Internet for less cost than a thirty-second ad on most television shows, a company's status quo gets in the way of clear thinking in favor of choosing the way things are as a safer bet. Despite knowing how rapidly everything is changing in technology and how we live in the digital world, more executives respond to me with status-quo thinking. A few get it, and that's why half of the world's top brands now possess this new digital asset (much more on this in chapter 2). There are countless entrepreneurs and people with new ideas who have been faced with the resounding "no" of the status quo.

Those inside an organization who don't want anything to change will reject new ideas summarily, largely based upon fear of failure. They don't want their territories, responsibilities, or budgets to change—or any aspect of their current comfort zones. Understandably, so, mind you. We who have it good like to keep it that way. I even had one high-level executive at one of the biggest companies in the world straight out say, "We don't like change." Sorry, but change is all we can count on these days. Change is mandatory and will happen whether you want it to or not. Things will continually change. Companies must continually change, particularly when it comes to digital. We can balance that out with some things we can count on or some amount of stability to keep us feeling safe, but every company must be in a state of continual evolution and change.

Remember these companies? CompUSA, Hostess, Borders, Pontiac, Woolworths, E. F. Hutton, and K B Toys? They are all out of business.

## PARADIGM SHIFTS OFTEN SEEM UNLIKELY

* "Who the hell wants to hear actors talk?" (Henry Warner, Warner Bros., 1927)

* "Sensible and responsible women do not want to vote." (Grover Cleveland, 1905)
* "Flight by machines heavier than air is unpractical and insignificant, if not utterly impossible." (Simon Newcomer, a noted astronomer, 1902)
* "The phonograph is of no commercial value." (Thomas Edison, of his own invention, 1880)
* "Change is the law of life. And those who look only to the past or present are certain to miss the future." (President John F. Kennedy)

Change is hard, even for very innovative and entrepreneurial organizations. But if there's one thing history teaches us, it's that people are actually hungry for change. People want change. Think of the many products and services we use today. From smartphones to Uber, GrubHub, and OpenTable, from Google Maps to Google search and the prospect of the driverless car—people really do want these changes that help make life better, more convenient, and less expensive, or that give us better experiences.

Consumers rely on companies and leaders to provide the changes they want that move our society forward. But the status quo is easily the default setting for most of us. And for many executives and managers inside large corporations and even small start-ups, it's initially easier to say no to something and not make a mistake than say yes to an idea and make a mistake. Only the true leaders can discern how to calculate risk and when to make investments in possibilities.

If you are on a board or in the C-suite of a company, ask yourself how your leadership team responds to change and the idea of change. This is important, because you, more than anyone else, can actually set the tone and the culture of the organization.

Sometimes it's helpful to look at history and recognize paradigm shifts that might have been hard to see at the time. Check out this link from the *Today Show* on NBC in October 1994: https://www.youtube.com/watch?v=UlJku_CSyNg&feature=youtube. (Go to www.boardroom.solutions for all of the videos referenced in this book.) This was before the word *digital* meant anything at all.

Katie Couric says, "Can you explain what Internet is?"

Bryant Gumbel asks what the @ symbol means when he is asked to read "violence@nbc.ge.com"—"What, do you write to it like mail?" They had no idea in 1994 what e-mail or the Internet was or how it would change everything. Neither did most of us. But a few visionary leaders did, and they built a whole new industry that led to other new industries.

In 1980, AT&T (whose Bell Labs had invented cellular telephony) commissioned McKinsey & Company to forecast cell-phone penetration in the United States by the year 2000. The consulting giant's prediction of 900,000 subscribers was less than 1 percent of the actual figure—109 million. Based on this legendary mistake, AT&T decided there was not much future in these devices. A decade later, to rejoin the cellular market, AT&T had to acquire McCaw Cellular for $12.6 billion. By 2011, the number of subscribers worldwide had surpassed 5 billion, and cellular communication had become an unprecedented technological revolution.

Sometimes these miscalculations on opportunities cost companies billions when they try to catch up. In 1943, IBM's chairman said he thought there was a world market for about five computers. At the time, one computer filled a room, and he couldn't see much use for them. But Bill Gates and Steve Jobs did see the need and built the companies that would later chase IBM out of the computer business and into the consulting business. In the boardroom and in the C-suite, your job is to be willing to take some risks and see what others cannot yet see.

I could continue to cite examples of how the pace of change is accelerating and one invention after another that has changed all the rules of how we do business. You would likely agree that things are changing fast. But I guarantee you, if I presented a roomful of top executives with an idea about how they could transform their digital business, most of them would tell me that I'm wrong, why it wouldn't work, or why it wouldn't work for them. Again, for most people, it's safer and easier to maintain the status quo. You generally don't get fired for keeping things the way they are. What did they used to say—"You don't get fired for hiring IBM"? But maybe you should. It's risky to consider new possibilities. And the truth is, many new ideas do fail, initially. But they usually lead to what ultimately can be transforming.

Microsoft originally introduced the idea of web-based TV back in 1996, but it failed. It was later reinvented as MSN TV in 2001 but was outcompeted by Apple TV and shut down in 2013. In 1996, it was certainly easy to think that people wouldn't access the Internet through their TVs.

Sidewalk.com was introduced in 1997 as a personalized, online city guide. Just a little before its time, it was replaced by Google Maps, something none of us can live without today. Even in far-reaching corners of the globe and in poor economic conditions, access to a smartphone with technology changes everything.

## HOW DO COMPANIES LOSE THEIR EDGE?

If you're wondering how companies lose their edge over time and sometimes become obsolete, it's not hard to see the signs when you look at history. It shows us when and how the shift began toward short-term, street-value thinking, from which executive bonuses trickle down. In this transition, the value of long-term research and development and building intellectual assets on a global level has diminished. While a few beacons of hope, such as Amazon, Google, Microsoft, and Apple, remain important American innovators, far too many other companies have given in to short-term over long-term value.

For nearly a hundred years, from the late 1800s to the late twentieth century, corporations focused on research and development to drive global growth of their companies. They were all about change and growth, and these were valued. Long-term growth was valued, that is. It is what created modern civilization—the investment these companies made in the technology that we rely upon today and the conveniences that make our lives what they are. From diapers and soap to Harleys and computers and smartphones, innovation flourished.

By the 1980s, megamergers created a few behemoth organizations while also stifling some cultures. If you think that just because there are a lot of consumer products out there, they aren't all owned by the same few companies, think again.

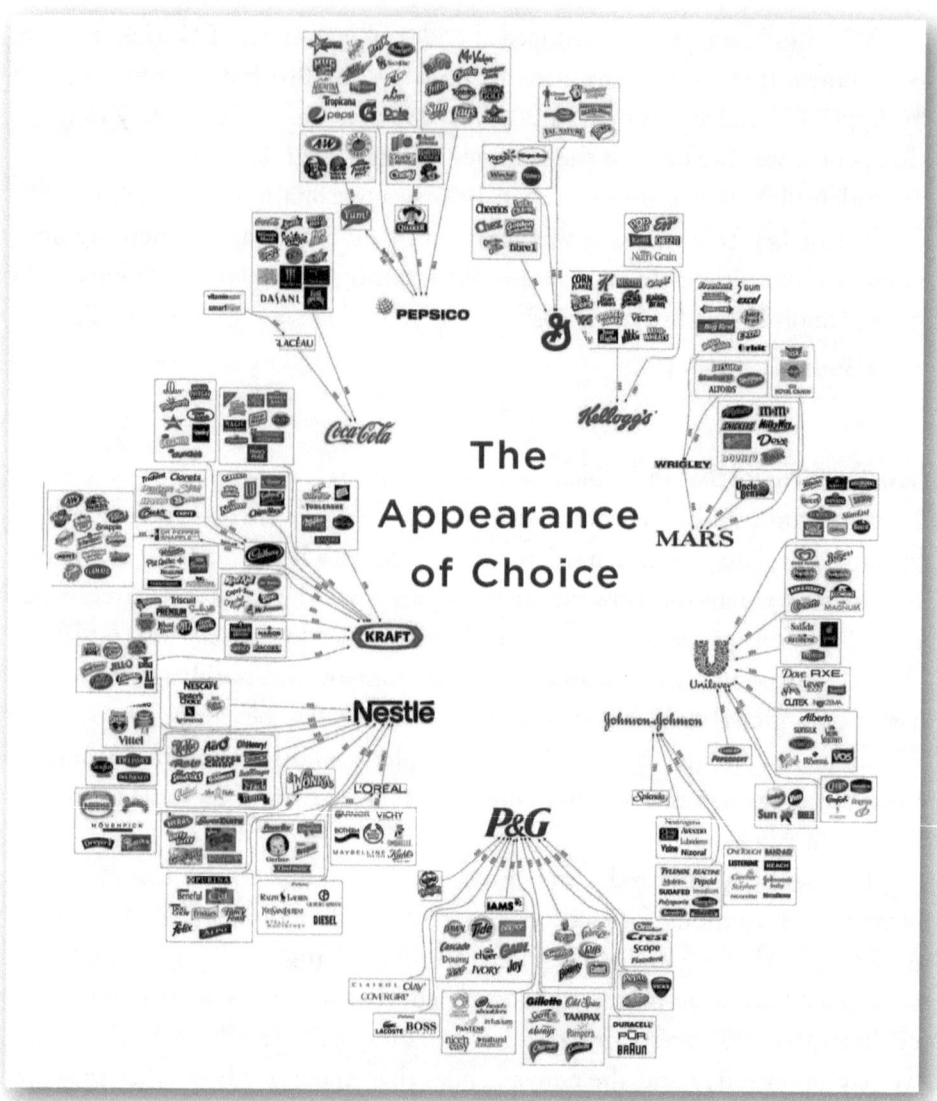

Fig. 1.3. The appearance of choice in the early 2000s

According to a study by the Ewing Marion Kauffman Foundation, between 1998 and 2004, the turnover of Fortune 500 companies was staggering. A full one-third of the companies listed in the 1970 Fortune 500 had disappeared by 1983 through acquisition, merger, or breaking into pieces.

It was also the age of Wall Street corporate greed, which moved us from a long-term, visionary management strategy to short-term strategy that leaves behind mistakes for someone else to manage. This is an unfortunate approach that has only accelerated in today's millennial mind-set: that one will only be at a company for a few years, not long enough to be there when his or her choices produce ramifications.

By the 1990s, technology and the Internet had taken over, and Wall Street had become driven by products and software that predicted stock prices, creating artificial assignments of value that was not real. Leading to a financial perfect storm, the 1990s offered a platform where individuals could buy stock online, and they invested most of their wealth in the market. Not by coincidence, cable companies had created a twenty-four-hour news cycle, and entire networks were dedicated to reporting minute-by-minute updates of markets around the globe. Combine institutional corporate greed and technology-driven algorithms for buying stocks with the average person reacting to a twenty-four-hour news cycle and the ability to immediately trade from anywhere with an Internet connection—and it's not hard to see why what came next did so.

Of course, when the financial markets crashed in 2008, most of us wondered how it had happened and how we could have let it happen. However, many had recognized the signals and predicted these collapses.

As we face the brave, new digital world ahead, it's important to begin with this lesson. While some level of short-term strategy is still necessary to respond to Wall Street's demand for public companies, someone in the boardroom or the C-suite needs to be thinking about the future of digital in your company. Change will happen. How is your organization investing in future opportunities and future thinking? How will you ensure that the status quo doesn't impede your company from inventing its future? How will you ensure the status quo doesn't cause you to become irrelevant in the changing digital world?

For inspiration, I always like to look at Bell Labs, often referred to as a hive of invention. In the early part of last century, Bell Labs invested in technologies that would drive the future of our society. It's responsible for the innovation that supports the digital age in which we now live. Without its long-term belief in the value of research and development rather than short-term market gains, we may not have been where we are today. Bell, after all, created the beginnings of technologies like the transistor, radio astronomy, UNIX operating system, C programming language, and C++ programming language, to name just a few. Free from day-to-day corporate demands, the work done at Bell Labs built the foundation for modern invention leading to phones, space exploration, the Internet, music distribution, cell phones, radio, television, and more.

When most of us think of who the Bell Labs of today might be, companies like Apple, Google, Amazon, and Samsung all come to mind. They are developing technologies and investing heavily in ideas that could lead to our future, a future most of us can barely imagine—like driverless cars or contact lenses that project images from the Internet directly onto our eyes (all of which Google has filed patents for).

While some of these companies are investing more into devices and tangible assets, they all rely on the Internet and its free, scalable use by not just their customers but also other entrepreneurs and companies who build ideas like Uber or GrubHub that further the consumer usage of their devices.

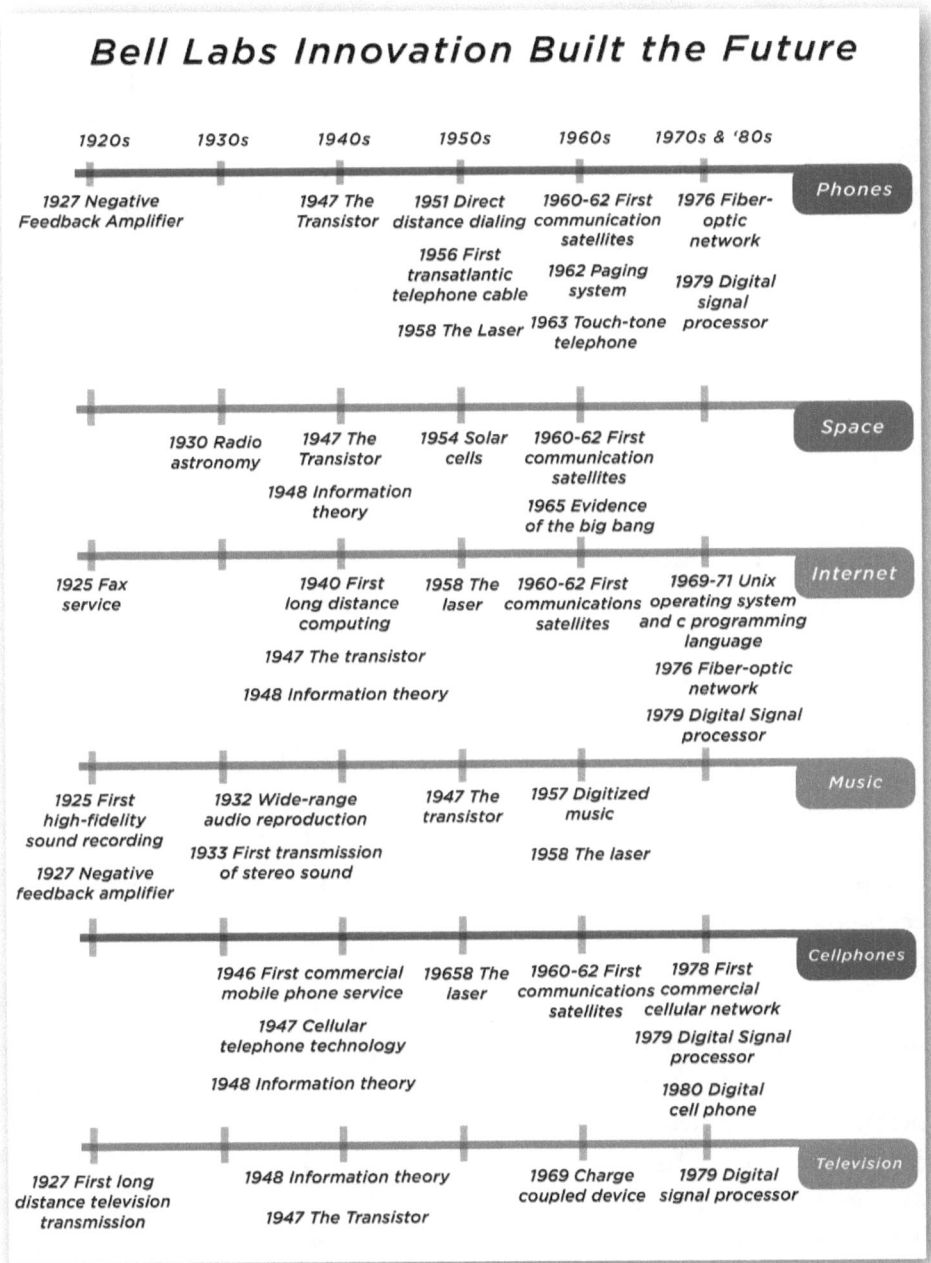

Fig. 1.4. History of Bell Labs

As we can learn from Bell Labs, innovation is about investing in new ideas, breaking down silos, allowing employees to take risks with budgets set aside for the purpose, tearing apart old assumptions, and thinking about the future. And then it's about owning those inventions for market dominance. Either you innovate and own it, or someone else will. What can you on the board do to move forward from the status quo?

**Leadership must set the tone.** Leadership must understand the value of building an innovation pipeline, capturing its new ideas, and then tracking them for protection and use as assets. It must be a strategic short- and long-term investment. It's important to pay attention to cultural change and provide incentives, both financial and recognition based, to facilitate a collaborative, knowledge-sharing environment that values intellectual assets as the end result.

**Process is essential.** Human beings are creative and innovative creatures. But to build upon new ideas, a process that facilitates the transformation from idea to reality and something of value is essential. Risk taking and failures must not just be allowed but celebrated when it comes to innovation. And budgets must be set aside for risks and failures.

**Technology and knowledge sharing are key.** Finally, using the right technology-based tools to capture ideas and share data and information across stakeholder groups is essential. All too often within large companies, multiple groups perform the same tasks, but with different data sets. The work must be centralized through knowledge sharing in a funnel to capture ideas, improve them, and then turn them into valuable assets.

Companies must do more with less and produce even greater return on investment faster to compete and survive today. But they can't sacrifice innovation and asset protection as a result. While Wall Street may value day-to-day performance and executives may strive for bonuses for it, the rest of us rely on companies to invest in our future. Where is the Bell Labs today that is creating the technology we need in thirty years? Is Google's spin-off, Alphabet, its predecessor? Only a handful of companies are even close. Savvy companies will invest in innovation pipelines and utilize technology of today for efficiencies to maximize the impact and return on investment.

To think about the future of your business in a digital age, you must be willing to proceed with the one assumption that all things will change. And once you are open to that reality, you can start to visualize and paint the future of your business.

If you have the ability to go beyond the status quo in your business when thinking about your digital future, then by all means, do it. Tell your team that you're going to consider new possibilities, and go into meetings with a new set of rules or assumptions. I've always liked the motto, "It's OK to fail, but fail fast." Remind those who prefer the status quo that in 2000, many companies didn't think that "Internet" thing would catch on and delayed in building out online presences, to their peril.

The status quo limits our thinking as individuals, as companies, and as a society. Turn off the status-quo mentality and open your team up for Step Two.

## STEP TWO: LOOK AT THE SIGNALS

To create the future of your digital world, your status-quo-free team can now look at the signals of change. First, it's important to consider how we, as individuals, live our lives every day. Whether you sell to businesses or individual consumers, you sell to people who make decisions. Understanding how people are living their lives will help you understand what they might want or need and how their behavior may shift in the digital world as a result of what is already happening and what's coming.

While the scales are certainly tipping in favor of the digital world, we're not in the Matrix yet. We do still function in a real and physical world. But there is now an intersection between how we live our digital lives with how we live our real-world lives. Understanding that intersection is a key signal for seeing the future.

Think about daily decisions we make. We constantly decide how to spend our time and money. Depending on your business, you want time or money—or both—from your target customer. There are countless in-depth studies and books about consumer behavior and what drives it, but if you think about your own life, you can easily see three drivers behind how you choose to spend your time or money in either the digital or real world:

1. Is it convenient?
2. Is it cheap (or free)?
3. Will I have a great experience, get something cool, be energized, or connect with other people in a meaningful way—so much so that it may be worth paying more for if I can afford it?

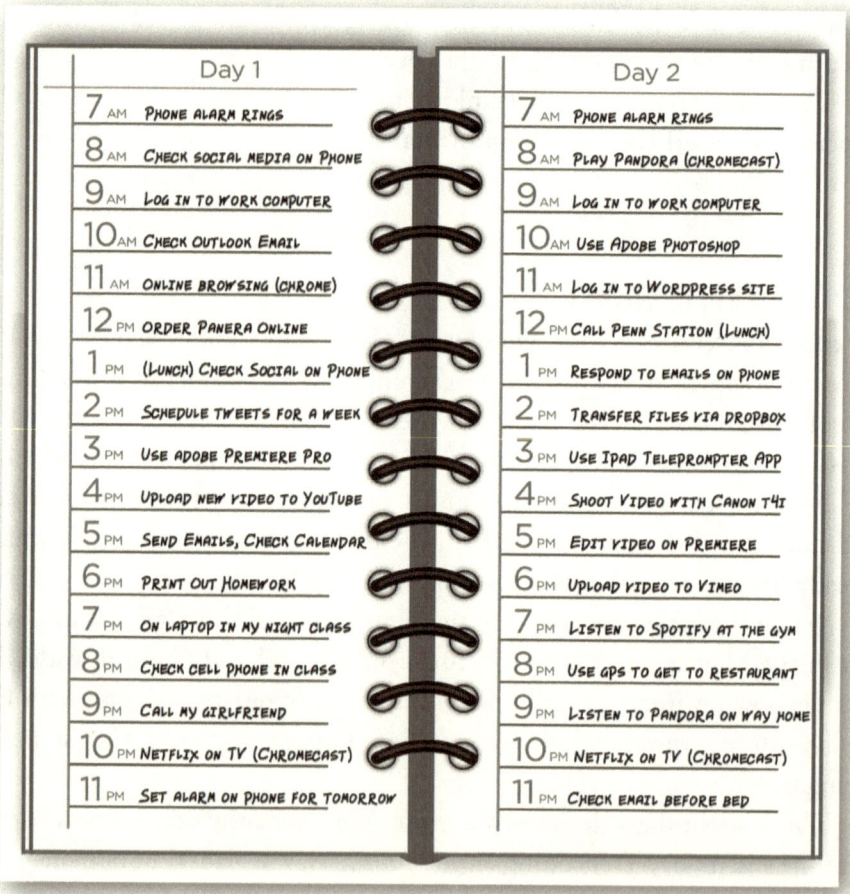

Fig. 1.5. Digital diary from one of my millennial team members who tracked his day and the motivation behind his behaviors.

Consider your daily routine from the time you get up to when you go to bed at night. Make a list of what you do in the real world and what you do in the digital world. Just for one day, keep track of it. While I illustrate just one example, I've pulled surveys and studies on how people live digitally to construct a high-level view of the digital world versus the real world.

If you do something on a computer, a phone, or a device or connect to the Internet through something, then list your action in the digital column. If you actually interact with another human being in person or do something in a physical location, then count that in the real-world column. You might be surprised how your day divides up.

I'll take you through a few of the big signals of how we now live digitally.

## OUR DIGITAL WORLD

Generally, what we do in the digital world is about having a convenient or free/inexpensive experience with one another and our brands. If we use this as a premise, then we know what types of experiences we need to create in the digital world. We need to make it easy and cheap (or free) to engage with our brands online.

**How we buy things.** Apple Pay may mean that eventually, we'll pay for everything with our phones. Starbucks already made that easy for our morning coffee with their app. Amazon Prime and Zappos's free shipping and returns have made two-day, free shipping a consumer expectation. Domino's actually has an emoji that a customer can text, and a pizza will show up at his or her door. It's easier to price, shop, and buy almost everything online—rather than in stores. Online groceries are already delivering to many areas. If we need to buy a new pair of shoes, why not surf Zappos, Amazon, or whatever your favorite store is online? Compare styles and sizes. Search for the best price on the same product. Most retailers offer free shipping and free returns, so if you're not sure about the size, order two and send one back. While the prices of our items may vary, we expect the digital-shopping experience to be convenient and free or inexpensive. And we expect retailers to send us our goods for free. This is why Cyber Monday has become bigger than Black Friday for retailers and why

Amazon could create its own consumer "holiday"—Prime Day. Soon, we may see Prime Day cards and gift cards among holiday-card selections.

According to an eMarketer report, e-commerce represented less than 1 percent of retail revenue in 1998 but today represents nearly 20 percent. Since 2002, e-commerce sales in the United States have quadrupled. With an average of a hundred million unique visitors per month, Amazon is the largest online retailer in the United States.

And we expect a great experience in our digital-shopping world. We may not get the thrill of walking home with packages, but we want to feel the joy of what we purchase, which is why so many retailers add special touches in the packaging—a bag, a bow, tissue and a sticker—whatever makes us happy. This is the key to creating the digital-shopping experience of the future. While groceries have not yet been successfully delivered outside of urban areas, the future will likely change this paradigm. Imagine if you could click a button to send a grocery list, just pull up at the store, and pick up your groceries, all neatly packed for you to take home. Or even have them delivered and waiting for you on your porch. Or—even better—already neatly put away for you in your pantry and refrigerator!

Algorithms will replace impromptu point-of-purchase shopping by making suggestions and offering recipes to go with our selections. This idea has already been filed in the patent office with applications related to such futuristic expectations. More retailers will develop personalized apps for your phone to customize your experience and know where you go in the store so that your online experience merges seamlessly with the one at home. The ability for you to track what you buy and "curate your closet" or "design your home" by combining items is the next phase of the Pinterest-board concept merged with big data. When will we stop using actual cash? Will bitcoins become the digital currency we rely upon in the future? Or will American Express, Visa, and MasterCard simply create a one-click shopping experience everywhere with chip technology or biometric technology?

The entire shopping experience—digitally—is becoming more and more convenient. Once companies master "convenient" and "free," the next step will be to create a better and more meaningful experience.

**How we are entertained.** Whether you use Apple TV, Roku, Amazon Fire, or Chromecast or have bought a smart TV, you either have watched or will watch in the near future content direct from the Internet cast to your flat-screen. Most of us have extensive libraries of digital entertainment on numerous devices so we watch what we want, where and when we want it. When we choose to be entertained on our tablets, phones, or computers, we are usually doing so because it's easy and free or inexpensive. What could possibly be more convenient? YouTube is free; lots of content is free—or very inexpensive. Music is ninety-nine cents a song, and movies are usually less than fifteen dollars for digital download, even as new releases. It doesn't cost us a lot, and more and more of the content we want is being offered for free.

The experience people have is often the connection to the content itself. Companies like Netflix, AMC, and HBO invest in top-tier content that connects in a meaningful way with an audience that then binge-watches when the next season is released. This is where the digital experience will start to change—how can you really deeply engage with your target audience through content? (I'll cover this extensively in chapter 7.)

For advertisers, it means that the old, linear style of running ads in a sequence while viewers watch TV may no longer work. Instead, ads will be programmatic and purchased by machines or embedded and tied to you watching something specific; this will change the multibillion-dollar buying behavior of advertisers. Companies can offer it conveniently. Companies can charge more for it if they create a better experience. And if companies find ways to deepen the experience, they have new opportunities and can see the signal of where entertainment is headed: 3-D, 4-D—what else is there?

Facebook's Oculus is trying to take us there, inserting us into a virtual-reality experience. The way we're entertained in the future will be a long way from how most senior executives and board members grew up, watching a TV with three, maybe four, channels and something called *TV Guide* being mailed to their homes to let them know what was on that week.

In the last five years, our consumption of Internet content has grown by 105 percent versus losses in almost all other media.

**How we work.** Even work has become digital. Most of us spend hours in e-mails, online sharing spaces, online meetings, or video chats, spanning hours across the globe. We can work remotely anywhere in the world and live where we want. Video and web conferencing via Skype or GoToMeeting makes it easy. Companies can even find services online without having to hire employees. Using Elance, Craigslist, or Freelancer.com, many can work almost exclusively online.

It's convenient because it means one can work from home when a child is sick or to avoid traffic. Think of the amount of time you save if you don't have a commute to and from an office—and the time you save by not chit-chatting in the office kitchen. And, for the most part, much of the technology that makes this possible is now inexpensive or free. Skype is free and quickly becoming the preferred means of international calling.

With all these time-saving devices, you'd think we'd have a lot more time for other things, but most people's number-one complaint is that they don't have enough time. Is there an opportunity there?

**How we connect.** Our social worlds continue to migrate into the digital world as Facebook, Twitter, Instagram, and so many others make it easier to interact with our friends in social networks or by group texting rather than over the phone or in person. You can communicate one-on-one or one-to-many; take your choice. It's certainly convenient. We can do it from any device, anywhere. It's usually free or cheap. All these Internet companies know the motto, "If you build it, make it free so the people will come." They need to build a critical mass, make it cool and get the people there, and then figure out how to make money. So all these social sharing sites are free. People use them because they are cool, the next big thing, and because they are convenient and free.

But is it a great experience? Are we just in the infancy of how we experience social connections online? So many flock to their social spaces to be heard, to matter, and to connect. How can that experience be better? That's the future of social connections online—a better experience, something more real.

**On the go.** Uber has made it easy to get a cab; GrubHub, easy to order food; OpenTable, to make reservations; Google Maps, to help us find our way. The list of apps that make our lives easy is never ending. Even dating has become an app function with Tinder. Whether we want to book a flight, change our seat, or kill time with a game, everything is at our fingertips on screens. Companies have figured out that if consumers consistently do one thing with them online, they need an app to make it easy. And then if they can create something that's fun or easy to do online, all the better.

Apps are sometimes free or not very expensive. Companies generally give them away to capture data about what we're doing. (When people finally understand that they have paid the price for this free technology with their privacy, will they care or change their behavior? Unfortunately, probably not.)

We've become accustomed to this tap-the-screen approach on our mobile devices. When we sit down at our desks to really work on something or want to spend more time researching, we'll click on a browser and search more traditionally. If you've cut the desktop computer from your life, you may still find yourself plugging into a larger screen at work or at home—which is where you are more likely to use a browser. Understanding this behavior trend is an important signal depending upon what experience your company wants to create for a customer digitally.

**How we get health care.** Even our health care is done more and more online. Before we go to a doctor, we look up our symptoms on WebMD or any of numerous other health-care sites. We look for people with similar situations and read about their experiences. We can order many supplements or drugs online. Our doctors require us to fill out forms online before we come to our appointments so that they no longer have to, and we put pages and pages of our most personal and private health information into a cloud-based system that we hope is secure. And once a doctor has prescribed a drug for us, we can continue to refill it automatically with a text or e-mail reply to our pharmacy—sometimes even have it delivered. It's all easy and convenient. No waiting for an appointment. No waiting for the doctor. No more waiting, period. We get what we want, when we want it, for day-to-day medical needs. But when something bad happens, we need a doctor, and we need one in person—which is when the digital world is no longer enough. Understanding these types of distinctions are the signals needed to predict how your company may need to adapt in the future.

**How we manage our money.** Online banking has been around for years but has recently become more and more secure. We can deposit checks by taking pictures of them. We can buy and sell investments from apps on our phones. We can apply for loans and sign documents, all online. We can move and access money all with a few clicks on a screen. It's all very convenient, and usually these services are offered at no charge, though our costs are probably hidden in other fees. We expect this of our banks. We want to pay all our bills and manage administrative tasks quickly and easily from the comfort of our homes.

When we do all of these things, we expect them to be easy, convenient, and usually free (or at least inexpensive). This is what the digital world has done for us. It has made our lives completely convenient and easy. It has done this all with limited costs to us, other than, of course, our privacy and the costs of the devices we cherish and purchase (often replacing them frequently with new models to stay on the cutting edge of all these great convenient and free digital experiences).

According to an Intel research study, today, the number of networked devices equals the global population, and in the future, it could be double that. The vast amount of time we spend in these digital spaces will continue to increase, not decrease, as devices get better at providing sight and sound so that it can become real. Heard of virtual reality or augmented reality? It's here. Speaking of real, when we lift our heads up from those devices, what do we do?

## OUR REAL WORLD

When we do leave our safe and comfortable digital enclaves and decide to interact with other live human beings, we want something more than just convenient and free or cheap. In fact, we generally expect experiences to cost more in the real world because we expect them to be better.

**Shopping.** If we actually bother to get in our cars or go to stores, we do so for a reason. We want to touch and see what we want to buy. We might need it right away and can't wait for shipping (hence Amazon's attempt at providing same-day drone delivery). We might want someone to help us make a selection (though that is happening online more and more). We are looking for experiences worth our valuable time and energy to get us to the stores and to look past the inconvenience of having to wait our turns to check out or for employees to let us into dressing rooms or help us—rather than the digital checkout.

In fact, some brick-and-mortar stores may create such fast-and-easy checkouts in the future. We might choose one store over another because it offers more convenience or because one is more or less expensive than the other. But we are really looking for experience when we go there—something that can't be delivered online. This is why Williams-Sonoma offers cooking classes and why every department store flags us down to try new fragrances, get free facials or makeovers, and watch fashion shows. This is why so many retailers are adding coffee bars, cafés, and places for us to continue the shopping experience. This is why Apple and Microsoft have turned their retail environments into experiences. It's certainly not convenient or cheap to do anything significant in the Apple Store, but it is an experience.

**Restaurants and cafés.** Of course, food has to be consumed in the real world. We can choose to order it online and have it delivered or pick it up, but when we go out, we are looking for an experience. For example, when we get our coffee at Starbucks, we certainly want it to be convenient (hence the drive-through), but we are likely also looking to feel the energy and vibe of the actual place and feel hot cups of coffee in our hands on a cold morning. The better the experience, the more we're willing to pay for it. We can't feel energy when we're at home…or can we? We can't have the restaurant experience from our computers—at least not yet.

Understanding what drives this part of our thinking and decision-making is the experience. The sights, smells, sounds, and energy from a physical place are not yet replicable online, and online probably never will be close to experiencing it in person. And restaurants and cafés can find important intersecting points to continue the experience in the digital world to bring us back to the real world, where we eat in restaurants. Retailers lure in shoppers with scents and smells that create memories of experiences. How will that carry into a digital world to keep us coming back?

**Travel.** We have to experience travel in the real world, too. But airlines, trains, hotels, and the travel industry have made it easy to make all our plans and bookings online. From the convenience of our homes, we can read all about every aspect of our trips. We can book and pay for everything in advance, having read real reviews form other live people (or so we think). Once we start our journeys, however, the experience is all real. But, if something goes wrong, the digital world is there to save us. Change our seats, our flights, our reservations; upgrade our rooms; even check in early, all from our devices—smart travel companies are intersecting the real and digital worlds in powerful ways. They know that when something goes wrong, we need help to fix it fast, and they have created digital tools to help us have that better experience.

Even getting from place to place is about the experience, whether it's by car, train, or plane. When we venture out, we decide if we're willing to pay more to be less inconvenienced and have better seats, food, and service.

**Entertainment.** We can watch movies on our phones, but going to theaters with the big screens, surround sound, and energy of a lot of other people, plus authentic movie popcorn, creates an entirely different experience—one we're willing to pay more for than in the convenient digital world. A concert is different, because we can actually feel the music as much as we can hear it and see the performance. We can feel the energy of the people around us. We can take in the theater itself and experience something completely differently than online.

**Work meetings.** Occasionally, we do find that we need to meet with people in person to work effectively. When it's important, when the experience matters, we invest in the time and money to be there. Sometimes seeing another person across the table—reacting to his or her real-time facial expressions and cues, pointing to documents in front of you or on the screen, adapting and responding, and, most important, showing that it matters enough to show up—can make or break a deal. We can find points of common ground, laugh, and connect in person—it's so much more valuable. Conferences provide the opportunity to network and build relationships. We're seeking that opportunity to build those relationships in a deeper way than we can sometimes build them online, creating opportunities both in the real and the digital worlds to connect these two types of experience.

**Social gatherings.** Most of us do still like to gather with our friends or families in person and socialize. What's so great about that experience? Why can't it be fully replicated digitally…or can it? Certainly, tools are there to bring people from around the world together, digitally, in the same room. For years now, at my home, we share a glass of wine with family members across the globe via Skype on a big flat-screen in our living room. We sit on the couch and talk to our family and friends as though they were in the room. But they aren't in the room, and it isn't quite the same.

Understanding what it is about the in-person experience versus the digital experience and thinking through these signals help us see how to build the digital world for the future of your company.

**Education.** While online learning has taken huge leaps forward, and adults frequently use online learning opportunities for the convenience of it, most parents are still looking to send their children to physical schools. In fact, many of us go to painstaking efforts and expense to ensure our children have the best possible experiences academically, socially, and culturally while getting their educations. In reality, our kids could probably learn all the lessons online, but the experience of being there with other people matters.

**Bridging the divide.** Companies now have to bridge the gap between the real and digital worlds, and they use mountains of data to help them do so. A *Harvard Business Review* article from 2014 states, "To consumers, the real and virtual worlds are one. The same should go for your company…Here we are a quarter century into the digital revolution, yet many companies still agonize over whether to invest significant resources in digital capabilities."

When we enter the real world, we expect free Wi-Fi so we can continue to go into and out of our digital worlds at our pleasure. If your company is a brick-and-mortar business, your managers need to know what people want when they turn up, and you need to continue the experience digitally. If your company is strictly an internet basedbusiness, your managers need to understand how your customer intersects with the real world as well as your digital world. These are all important considerations for the future of digital in your organization and essential to predicting the future of your business in a digital world.

The signals are all there in the digital world. Using those signals requires understanding how we live our lives in the real world and in the digital world. It requires understanding what's missing as we transition from one to the other and then applying it to your business and where your company fits in the matrix of it all. Every signal that you need to help you see where your company fits in the future digital world is there.

## STEP THREE: MAP YOUR DIGITAL WORLD AND PAINT THE FUTURE

Ready to know the future? Do you want to wait and read about it in the headlines, or do you want to create the digital future for your business? Now that you've thought about the digital signals, map out the digital world of your customers, your competitors, and your vendors. Understand how they live their lives in the digital and real worlds and where you fit in that mix.

Ask yourself these questions and use the answers to identify how your digital world should work:

1. What do you need to provide your customers as they transition from the digital to the real world and back again?
2. How do you make that transition more convenient, cost less, or become a better experience?
3. What should your digital world look and feel like?
4. What will your customers want from you in their digital life?

This is how to build a digital strategy that will work for you—by understanding the signals of change and where you fit in that landscape.

How people search and navigate the massive digital world has changed fundamentally. It's no longer about gaming search algorithms; it's about something much bigger. Look for the signals of how people need and want to engage with you in your digital world. Learn what they want before they know they want it, and you'll have a winning digital strategy. A key is to understand the intersection of data and then develop it into digital intelligence. In this graphic, I show the three big data points to gather. First, what's happening in mobile or Internet of things and social spaces? Second, what sort of online search and traffic data do you have? Now, combine these with trends in online consumer spending. In the intersection of this diagram is Digital

Intelligence. (I'll cover it in more detail in chapter 8 but wanted to introduce the topic early.) If you're on a board or in the C-suite of your company, your management team should be able to understand how Digital Intelligence is driving strategy and critical thinking. This means that you'll gather data and understand all facets of the digital experience and the interconnection of all of the pieces.

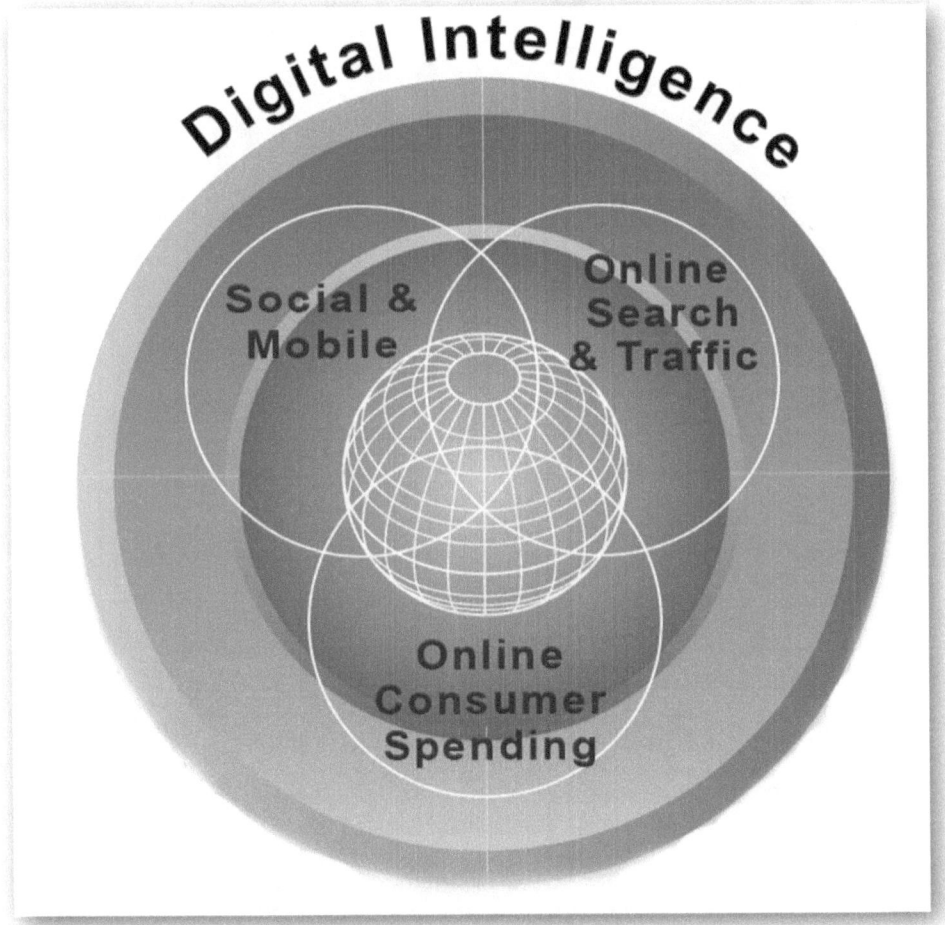

Fig. 1.6. Digital Intelligence

This is the start to your Digital Intelligence. It's just one piece of the puzzle you need to put together. Once you have gathered all the digital intelligence about your company, it's time to do what I refer to as Digital Mapping®. It is a competitive analysis, but of the digital experience for your consumers, plotted on a map to help you see it graphically. Figure 1.7 below shows how this works, but, again, I cover the concept in much more detail later.

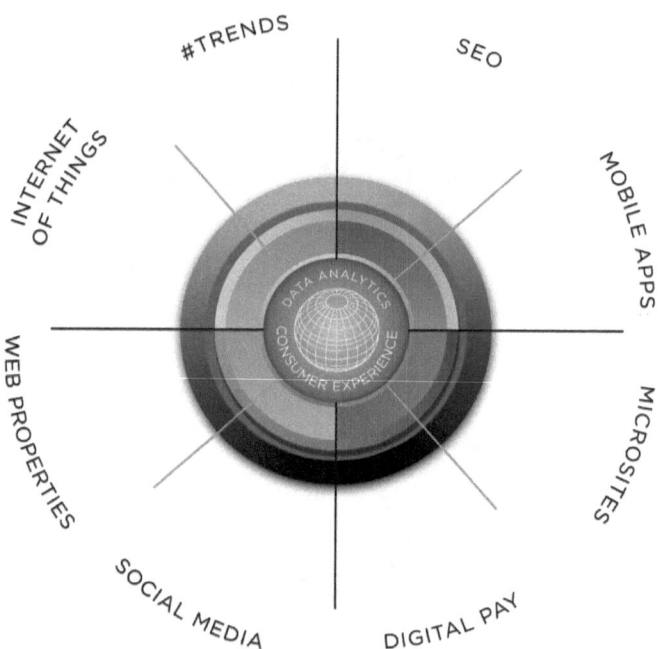

Fig. 1.7. Digital Mapping®

The big question for your board is, is your company preparing a holistic digital strategy based upon a keen understanding of all of the forces impacting your digital world? All of the components of the digital map—search-engine optimization, mobile apps, microsites, digital pay, social media, web properties, the internet of things and #trends—all create the digital experience. You can plot your map after going around your digital world and understanding what experiences exist there and how they connect.

**Want to know the signals of change in your organization?** You must first understand your target customers. Consider what their digital experience is like. Ask yourself questions about your target customers. For example:

What matters to them about their digital experience? Based on our discussion so far, you already know what the answers are

- Convenience
- Low or no cost
- Quality of experience

Other important questions include the following:

➤ How do your target customers engage in the digital world?
    - How do they buy things?
    - How are they entertained?
    - How do they work?
    - How do they connect to others in social spaces?
    - How do they use apps or the Internet of things?
    - How do they access health care?
    - What do they search for online?
    - How do they manage their money?
    - What matters most to them when they do these things?

➤ How do they engage in the real world?
    - What gets them to go out to shop in the real world? What do they want when they get there? How does it connect back to their digital world?

- Where do they go out to eat or for coffee? What experiences are they looking for in those places? What keeps them going back?
- How do they travel? When and where do they go? How do they pay for it? What do they need while they travel?
- What entertainment do they seek out in live experiences?
- How do they work? What's important when they work? What gets them out of the office or the home?
- When do they gather with friends and family? Where? What's important when they do? What can you do to make that better?
- How do they educate themselves and their children? What matters to them about education?

➤ How will your competitors address your customers?
- How might they outperform you or give customers more of what they need?
- What about big technology companies—how will changes made by Google, Amazon, Facebook, Microsoft, and others impact your industry?
- What companies could start providing the same products or services or future products and services to your customers?

In addition, as digital makes its way into the boardroom, these are the key questions you need to ask your C-suite and managers:

➤ How do we ensure that the status quo doesn't block ideas?
➤ How are individuals incentivized to think about the future of the company?
➤ What may be in place that stifles creative thinking?
➤ How do we balance harvesting existing businesses with investment in the future?

➤ Is there a "safe" place for innovative activities to occur at the leadership level?
➤ Are we insulated from what's actually happening in our company?
➤ How often do we stop and think about how the changing digital world will impact our business?
➤ Do we have a digital committee on our board to ensure that silos are not missing key signals and to help provide us guidance on these accelerating trends?

The C-suite and the board have unique roles. Your direction can set the tone for how the organization operates. I've seen many instances where, down deep in the organization, strategies or mandates are misunderstood. There are many components to digital transformation. Ready to dig into them?

In the coming chapters, I dig deeper into the components of the digital map wheel (Figure 1.7) and how your company can create a digital future by carefully thinking about all of them:

**Web properties.** I'll cover the big bang no one has heard and tell you how the entire online experience will change. Will you be ready?

**Cybersecurity.** This critical issue touches every company and all facets of the digital map. I'll provide more details on what you should know, how to be prepared for the inevitable, and how each component of the wheel could expose you to attack.

**Search.** I'll cover the SEO (search-engine optimization) segment of the wheel and explain how SEO has worked in the past, how it shaped the way we navigate the Internet, and how it will change in the future.

**Social media.** I'll cover how social media impacts your customers, as well as what you should and shouldn't do on social media.

**Mobile, apps, and the Internet of things.** In this chapter, I'll cover what's happening in mobile and app usage and how the Internet of things will transform all of our companies.

**Content will always be king.** Key components of your digital wheel are microsites and #trends—all of which relate to the content you create. Content will always be a critical component of digital.

**Digital Intelligence.** I'll present research on how you tie this all together into digital intelligence you can use. I'll include external factors you may not have considered in the past, like looking at patent filings to predict the future digital world and know when you are facing future threats.

I write each chapter in terms of what your company should be doing and the considerations for you as an individual director or executive. In the final chapter, I close out with the state of digital in the boardroom, including recommendations for boards in integrating digital into the boardroom and how senior leadership can set the tone and look for signals of change to be prepared for the digital future. The fundamental principle for understanding digital in the boardroom is to consider your digital world as a map. When fully connected, all of the components intersect with data analytics and the consumer experience at the core. The role of the board is to oversee this strategy to ensure that your company is not exposed to risk or threats that impact shareholders. In this book, I'll address each component of the digital map, but your digital strategists should be able to plot a strategy and show you how it creates a connected and comprehensive digital world for your company.

## KEY TAKEAWAYS FROM CHAPTER 1

* Change in digital and cybersecurity is constant, and you must continually learn and evolve as a company and as an individual. Start with the assumption that change is the law of life.
* Turn off the status-quo mentality in your company. Be aware of it and specifically how it can lead to catastrophic threats or missed opportunities.
* Be mindful of the signals of change in our digital world. How do your customers migrate in and out of the digital world? How do you

as an individual move from one to the next? The signals of change and what will exist in the future are all there; you just need to put the pieces together.

* Understand and map your digital world so that you can understand how your customers interact with you and what they will need and want in the future. This knowledge leads to more effective management and oversight of digital in the boardroom.

*Chapter 2*

## THE BIG BANG NO ONE HEARD

Someday, future business leaders may ask you if you remember when our Internet universe exploded from twenty-three top-level domains to more than a thousand, creating endless, new natural-language possibilities in the digital world. It happened in 2014 and 2015. Did you hear about it? Probably not, because it was a quiet revolution of the most powerful communication tool of our time. The average person doesn't know what a domain name is or how it's relevant to Internet navigation, let alone what a top-level domain is or how it could change so many things. So, why should you care that we got a whole lot more top-level domains?

Other than a few industry insiders and intellectual property lawyers, most marketing and C-suite executives know very little about this expansion of the Internet. The status-quo advertising and marketing editors didn't get it or understand it. Most mainstream media didn't cover it, and those that did generally viewed it negatively. Marketing conferences didn't talk about it. If executives heard of it at all, they were unclear on the impact and relegated any concern about it to their lawyers to ensure they were protected. A few CEOs knew about it and understood it, and their companies made bold moves as a result. What's most important for you in the boardroom to understand is that, for the first time in the history of the Internet, companies can own their brands as top-level domains and can create exclusive digital neighborhoods unlike anything we had in the dot-com era.

What's this all about, and how will it impact your company? Let me break this down for you with a brief history. The Internet became mainstream back in the 1990s, resulting in what is commonly referred to as the dot-com boom. When the Internet and websites first became available, there were only a few possible top-level domains available—what I refer to as channels of the Internet. You probably have heard of those. They include dot-gov for government websites, dot-org for nonprofit websites, and dot-edu for educational websites.

Fig. 2.1. Four channels of the Internet

Then there was dot-com, which became the catchall pile for essentially everyone and everything else on the Internet. Every single person and business that created a website chose a dot-com, whether a Fortune 500 blue-chip company or a counterfeiter, a typo squatter, or a porn site. Everyone seemed to want to be in the dot-com space. It became the gold standard of naming on the Internet.

Many businesses, particularly big Fortune 500 companies, were slow to recognize the impact of the Internet in the 1990s. They didn't understand that it would change everything, assuming it was a fad and that no one would trust this Internet thing. They didn't know that a domain name could be important as a digital address. And because they waited, a new industry of speculators quickly formed—the domain investors. New domain names cost ten to fifteen dollars a year, creating a price point at which almost anyone could buy up hundreds of domain names and then later sell them at exorbitant markups if they had something a company really wanted.

This was the Wild West of the early web, and there weren't any laws on the books yet to stop people from buying up existing brand names. In addition to domain investors buying up really great keyword names and broad categories—everything from baby.com to wine.com, from realestate.com to newyork.com, and from lighting.com to razors.com—they could also acquire big brands or typo versions of big brands and later charge the real brands who wanted them tens of thousands to hundreds of thousands and even millions of dollars. Over time, domain-name speculating became a reasonable business proposition.

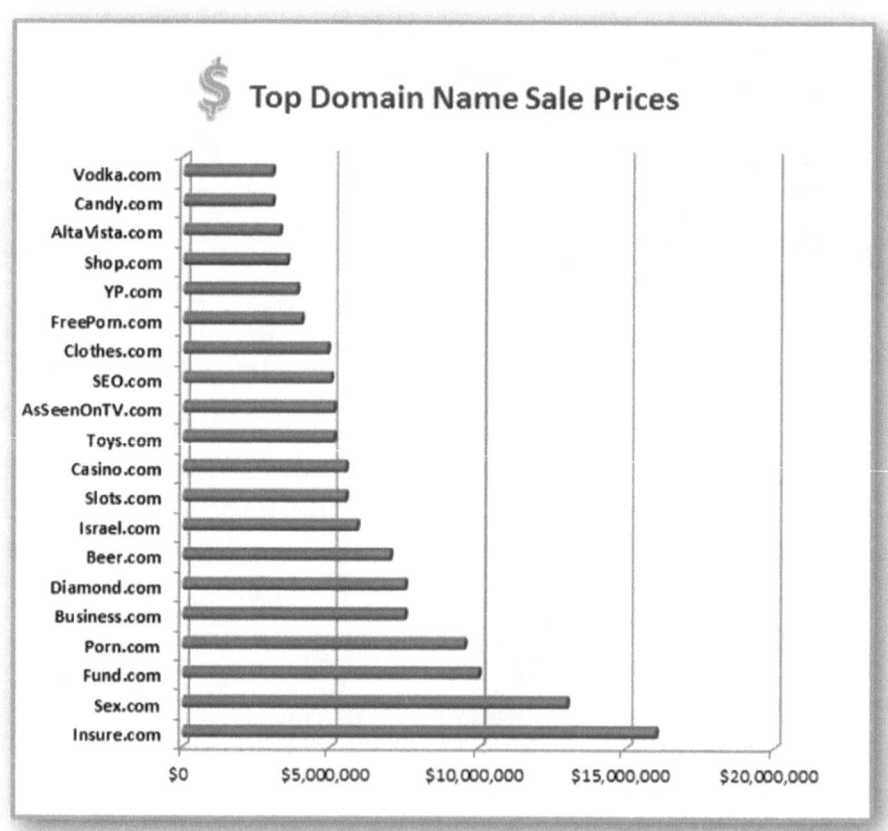

Fig. 2.2. Top domain-name sales

Whatever ad or branding agencies created, the domain-investor industry had already acquired the desired domain names, and companies quickly learned to shell out big bucks because they had already invested too much in their product names. It created a negative view of the domain-name industry for many in corporate America.

Of course, sometimes a domain bought from someone else turned out to be a better deal than it first seemed. Uber, for example, purchased uber.com from Universal Music Group for 2 percent of the company. Once Uber had funding, it bought the domain name for $1 million from Universal and recovered its shares. Universal probably thought $1 million for a domain name was a good bet, but it would have been better off hanging on to those early Uber shares.

Fast-forward to 2012, when the Internet Corporation for Assigned Names and Numbers (ICANN)—allowed companies to apply to operate top-level domains in an open application period, the first of its kind in the history of the Internet. The interest was overwhelming. ICANN received nearly two thousand applications to operate new top-level domains in four general categories:

### The Facts: During the ICANN 2012 Window

- 1,930 Applications were submitted
    - 116 are IDNs comprising Chinese, Arabic, Cyrillic
    - 1409 unique strings to launch in the next 2 years
    - 230 strings in conflict (751 applicants)
    - 47% from North America
    - 35% from Europe
    - 16% from Asia Pacific
    - Less than 2% from Latin America & Africa
- 50% of Interbrand's Top 100 Global Brands applied.
- 36 of the Fortune 100
- ICANN is likely to open a second window to acquire top level domains in 2-3 years.
- ICANN earned more than $350 million in fees.

Fig. 2.3 The facts of the new top-level domains

1. Generics for terms like dot-dad, dot-family, dot-pizza, and dot-solutions—literally more than a thousand possibilities (see Appendix for a complete listing).
2. Brands—representing half of Interbrand's top-one-hundred global list—applied to operate their own top-level domains. This would be like dot-macys, dot-tiffanys, dot-bmw, dot-sky, and dot-mlb.
3. Various cities or geographic regions like dot-nyc, dot-vegas, and dot-london, and some communities, such as dot-pharmacy or dot-bank.
4. The most impressive, bold moves were by the big technology companies. Examples include Google, which applied to operate 101 new top-level domains, and Amazon, which applied to operate 76 new top-level domains. Hundreds of other big brands applied to operate their own top-level domains, but this was primarily out of fear rather than strategic and visionary thinking about the future. Most of these top-level domains are now live, though only a few companies have started to use them or migrate from their dot-coms.

While there are many benefits to operating a top-level domain as a Dot Brand or using a new domain name to build out microsites or specific campaigns as exclusive digital neighborhoods, the fact that powerhouse companies like Google and Amazon made such bold moves should certainly be enough to get the attention of most senior executives and have them ask the all-important question: Why did they do this? Do they know something we don't know?

In the boardroom, understanding how Internet policy impacts your company should not just be left to your company's technology and legal groups. If you rely on the Internet to run your company, then what happens in Internet policy directly impacts your company. Changes could impact the very viability of your company and certainly your vision for the future.

In this chapter, I'll explain in detail what's happening in this expansion of the Internet and why it matters so much to every company. I'll start with how other paradigm shifts occurred and how this fits into a natural pattern of shifts. I'll put this in context with other current major digital transformations and show you examples of how it will impact and benefit consumers and businesses around the globe. I'll then provide a few basics about how it all happened and how you could know about these changes in the future.

In the Beginning There Are Always Just a Few Options

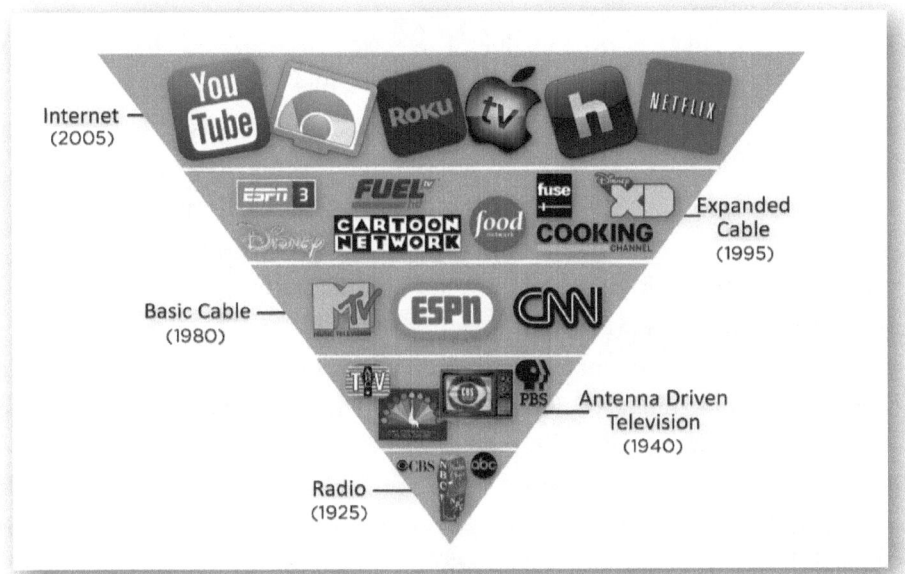

Fig. 2.4. History of radio and television

Nearly a century ago, a new technology burst onto the scene, providing people with live access to content, entertainment, news, and information. It was a breakthrough at the time, called the radio. While radio technology had been around for some years, by 1925, it was put into an affordable product that became the focal point of many living rooms. Families would gather around this large piece of furniture and listen in to the news of the day or be entertained by content and programming produced by three networks: ABC, CBS, and NBC (in the US market).

These three networks continued on throughout World War II as trusted brands in the American household. By the 1940s, the television was replacing the radio as the focal point of the living room. As families now gathered to watch favorite programs or news anchors, the same three channels remained trusted friends: ABC, CBS, and NBC.

Not everyone was enthusiastic: "Television won't be able to hold on to any market it captures after the first six months. People will soon get tired of staring at a plywood box every night" (Darryl Zanuck, movie producer for 20th Century Fox, 1946).

But time would prove the value of television. Not much changed in TV over the next thirty to forty years. Black-and-white TV evolved to color TV (this was device driven), and PBS was introduced in the 1970s (this was content driven). While local stations gained some programming ability, the American population relied upon ABC, CBS, and NBC for essentially all of its news and entertainment. At the time, no one knew that any more than three channels (with maybe the addition of a few weak broadcasts on VHF channels) was even necessary, or imagined what they might be missing.

I can only imagine what television executives at those networks thought when the idea of cable television was introduced. If we could go back in time and tell them about the Internet, streaming television, Netflix, and consumers bypassing ads or even choosing which ads they watch, those executives would have thought we were crazy. Even the major advertisers of the time likely believed things were just fine the way they were and that there was no need for more than a few channels. I can imagine them saying in the conference rooms of the 1970s and early 1980s, "Wouldn't that just be complicated? People will be confused and won't like it!"

But change did come, slowly at first and then rapidly accelerating. In the 1970s and 1980s, the concept of segmentation by interest was introduced, with basic cable now providing a twenty-four-hour news channel, twenty-four-hour sports channel, and twenty-four-hour music channel. Advertisers could actually target consumers based upon interests. And enthusiasts had channels dedicated to their interests.

By the mid-1990s, these specialty channels had expanded even further into first hundreds and then thousands of channels available for all types of interests from science fiction to food to home design to even reality television about tall people, short people, naked people, housewives of all sorts of cities, and, of course, the original reality family, the Kardashians.

By 2005, Internet channels were introducing the concept of streaming and on demand so that consumers could not only choose from thousands of niched programming themes, but they could also watch what they wanted, when and where they wanted, further complicating the market for advertisers desperate for attention from their target consumers. This, in particular, is an important shift because it parallels exactly what is happening with the Internet right now.

Remember the story of the beginning of the Internet in the 1990s that I shared at the beginning of this chapter? Because most companies didn't understand that the Internet was about to change everything, they didn't see the need to buy domain names and later paid the price. The same thing is about to happen again. Big companies are not paying much attention to this quiet Internet revolution because they don't see the future. And when they later want these assets, they will pay a premium, or perhaps the assets won't be available at all.

I have several more examples of paradigm shifts to share with you, but first, it may be helpful for you to understand who runs the Internet and who decides when these top-level domains can be issued.

In those early days of the Internet, the US government controlled these initial "channels," and the Department of Commerce administered dot-com (as in commerce). In 1993, the National Science Foundation (the federal agency charged with administration of the Internet since 1991) contracted with Network Solutions to assign domain names for dot-com, dot-edu, dot-net, dot-org, and dot-gov with annual registration fees of fifty dollars, respectively. In 1995, Network Solutions was acquired by Science Applications International Corporation for $4.8 million, and then in 2000, it was sold to VeriSign for $21 billion. Network Solutions had a monopoly on domain-name registration until 1999, when it was placed under ICANN's oversight. VeriSign continues to operate dot-com under a contract with the US Department of Commerce. Despite the irrational exuberance of the dot-com era and horror of the dot-com bubble, VeriSign has continued to watch over and protect dot-com, an important task.

The US government created ICANN, as a California nonprofit organization, to serve as the global policy-making body for the Internet. The goal was fairly straightforward: bring together stakeholders who have an interest in Internet governance and let them set policy for the Internet without government interference.

ICANN is a complex organization, and commentary on it is far beyond the scope of this book, but, needless to say, there are groups within ICANN that are represented by those parties that actually operate the Internet like registry operators (those that run the backend operations, like VeriSign) and registrars (those that sell the actual domain names, like GoDaddy) or Internet-service providers (those companies that give people access to the Internet, like Verizon, Comcast, Time Warner, or Cox).

And then there are groups who represent classes of people or organizations like intellectual-property owners, business owners, at-large members, academics, and noncommercial entities who care about civil liberties and similar issues, as well as a government advisory committee intended to reflect government viewpoints. Within the ICANN environment, policies are set that can change everything—like this Dot Brand program that allowed for a massive expansion of the Internet, or the potential transition of the oversight of ICANN from the US government to ICANN itself under the transition of the Internet Assigned Numbers Authority (IANA) function. IANA is what actually controls the domain-name system root zone (or base to the Internet) and the numbering system behind the Internet. This is actually really important, as it removes the contractual oversight from the US government that formed ICANN and places full trust and authority in ICANN to self-monitor and self-police, much like the United Nations. This is not something you should only find out about after it happens—you should know the impact it could have on all things digital before it happens.

In Eric Schmidt's book *The New Digital Age*, he warns of concerns about ICANN and countries around the globe wanting to operate their own Internet policies: "Governments will feel as if they're fighting a losing battle against an endlessly replicating and changing Internet, and balkanization will emerge as a popular mechanism to address this challenge." What happens in ICANN will determine how governments run their Internets and what policy impacts the Internet you rely on for your digital operations. Will Internet Isolationism replace a global Internet system? Do you do business in China, Russia, Brazil, India, or other countries that may not have the same Internet policies? You might want to know how governance of the worldwide Internet is changing as you consider the future of your digital business.

In the domain-name space from 1999 until 2014, a few other top-level domains were introduced, including dot-biz, dot-mobi, dot-travel, and dot-museum. Countries were also introduced as two-letter country codes, such as dot-us or dot-uk. Many country codes existed prior to the mainstream Internet days but officially formed as part of ICANN in 2003, when the Country Code Names Supporting Organization (ccNSO) was established.

Within the United States, none of these had an impact or stole any thunder from what was and remains the gold standard of web addresses, a good dot-com. But in 2012, that all changed. (My book *Domain Names Rewired* details this process and features interviews with leading executives from Fortune 500 companies predicting trends on what might happen because of this policy change and what it could mean.)

In that window of time, more than half the world's top brands applied to operate their own top-level domains, including the bold moves by Google and Amazon. And more than a thousand new top-level domains have now entered the Internet landscape, providing hundreds of choices and the potential for a paradigm shift in the naming space with options ranging from dot-solutions and dot-technology to dot-movie and dot-lol and dot-sucks.

Now, many of you in the boardroom may be asking, "Why do we need that? What does it do? What's the difference?" I understand completely that this is the initial reaction—as it likely was when cable was brought up to television executives. Before I delve deeper into the benefits of this new way of operating the Internet and its benefits to all of us, I'd like to take a look at a couple of other paradigm shifts for important context. But recognize this one important factor about digital in the boardroom: Internet policy is important. Decisions made by and about ICANN and IANA could impact the way the Internet is governed around the world. Digital is run by the Internet via devices. What happens at ICANN does matter in the boardroom.

Remember, as noted in chapter 1, when looking for signals about the future, it's not about one or even two things in isolation but the signals from all of the pieces to the puzzle. That's how we predict the future. In the boardroom, you aren't expected to use a crystal ball, but you are expected to oversee the company and be sure that your CEO and other key executives are thinking about the future. How the Internet is governed, what could change, and how it could change impacts pretty much every company on the planet.

So, what other signals should we look for? Why is this shift important? And, if it's so important, why isn't anyone else talking about it? I shared with you that the way we have accessed content from radio and television evolved into niched and fragmented cable and then to on-demand, Internet-based content. But what about other paradigm shifts? Think about telephone communication. It started with Alexander Graham Bell's invention of a device that allowed us to talk to people far away. The telephone became a household item for most families by the 1960s.

From that time, there weren't many changes. There were party lines, of course, at first, but eventually, every household had its own phone lines. Then the cords got a little longer, so folks could walk farther away from the phone, which was still attached to the wall in the kitchen. Then touchtone replaced rotary dials. But, other than that, for nearly fifty years, there weren't many changes to the traditional telephone. Eventually, antennas appeared, and we had spotty use of cordless phones. And, despite that fact that cell phone technology existed as early as the 1940s, it wasn't until the mid-1990s that the average person carried a cell phone regularly. Prior to that, only the wealthy had phones, and these were used in their cars; the phones were fairly large and were carried in big bags and cases.

By the early 2000s, just about everyone had a cell phone, and Verizon, Sprint, AT&T, and T-Mobile rushed to connect towers and provide service around the globe. Device makers like Apple, Samsung, and Microsoft rushed to provide better and better options. At an accelerating pace, smartphones took over, and now mobile is the marketing strategy of the day. Apps, geolocation tracking, and minicomputers drive behavior and make our lives easier than ever before, all at the touch of the screen.

### Digital in the Boardroom

We tailor our phones to what matters to us, and we connect with friends all over the globe from smartphones in our pockets—soon to be in our watches, connected to our homes, cars, and everything we touch. This same type of change is now happening on the Internet. At first, we were in dial-up mode, with only a few places to go or things to do on the Internet. Then a few more options showed up, but nothing dramatic. Now, the current expansion is like the introduction of the smartphone. From this silent explosion, many changes will follow. A similar story was true for computers. The acceleration happened at a slow pace, initially followed by rapid changes and near-universal adoption. In the 1940s, computers filled entire rooms. I previously mentioned that the chairman of IBM in 1943, Thomas Watson, said that he thought there was a world market for about five computers. It was this type of thinking in IBM's boardroom that led to the decision to allow Bill Gates to keep his software when he approached them about buying his computer. Bill Gates kept the rights to the software software. This is a perfect example of how boards are in the unique position to think about the future and ensure their companies are not throwing away important new ideas or assets.

One final example before looking specifically at what the differences are in the online experience of the past and the future: it's about how we send messages and packages.

In the beginning, we had the pony express, with an actual person on a horse riding across the frontier to deliver letters, messages, and packages. Morse code was also once used to send telegraphs and information. But the expectation was that getting any messages sent from a distance would take time. For centuries, messages were delivered at a snail's pace, without much innovation.

And then, in 1943, in the United States, the idea of the zip code was introduced. What's so important about this is that it was the first time in a post–World War II era that the concept of segmentation by where someone lived was possible. This was the dawn of the data industry, gathering information about people based upon where they lived. In fact, the introduction of zip codes created entirely new industries.

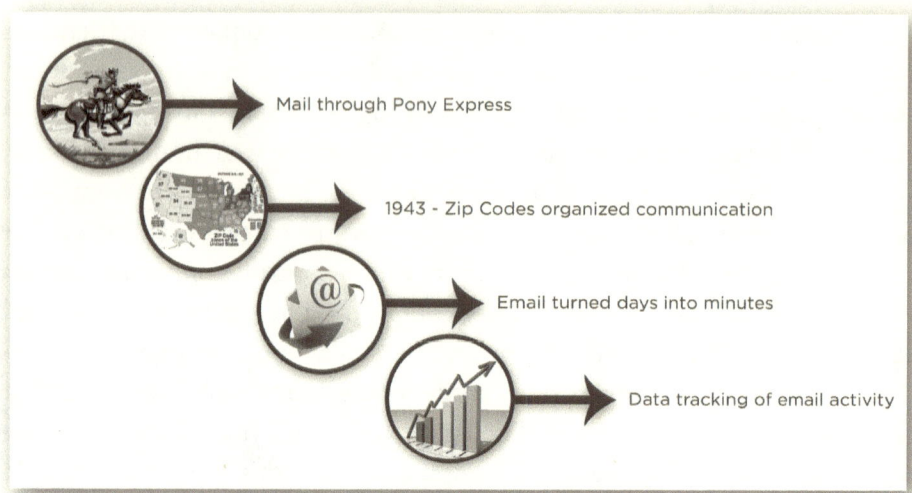

Fig. 2.5 Evolution of mail and data

The direct-mail industry was formed for companies to target zip codes or neighborhoods of consumers who comprised their targeted customers with marketing and sales materials and catalogs—oh, the catalogs! It was the very beginning of big data and understanding how to reach a target audience at home. This segmentation of mailing addresses started a transformation that would take another fifty years to fully shift. Zip codes allowed marketers to target their messaging, and companies like FedEx and UPS responded to this new opportunity. Who could have guessed that our appetite for segmentation and delivery of what we want would shape our society in the way it has in our digital world?

As with the other paradigm shifts I've discussed, decades went by in postal delivery with very few innovations or changes, but then when they hit, they hit quickly. When e-mail turned days of travel time into minutes to reach the intended recipient, it wasn't long before tracking how we all behave in a digital world created data that helped marketers make smarter decisions and engage with consumers in an entirely new way. Much like the silent expansion of the Internet, it happened quickly and without a lot of warning. Now, rather than waiting for us to request something, marketers use contextual intelligence to guess what we want next and serve it right up to us. And Amazon can deliver it for free in two days or less.

The common theme of these big paradigm shifts is that they all flow in a digital direction. The segmentation of mail that began with zip codes has evolved into digital segmentation that, in a very Big Brother kind of way, tracks what all of us are doing at almost any moment of the day: whom we talk to, what we buy, and even what we think when we post it all day long on social media—the tracking is at much more depth than just a zip code telling marketers where we live.

In other words, though each of these big paradigm shifts saw little innovation for decades, or even centuries in some cases, they all culminated in rapid development in the last ten to fifteen years to become more and more digital.

Now, companies must understand all facets of the digital environment and build out spaces tailored to what customers want and expect. It's not just about having a single domain name and a single website. The Digital Map and digital world is much more expansive than that today. The expansion of the domain-name space is one piece of this changing digital world, but it's an important one and clearly follows the logics behind other paradigm shifts. Consumer expectations have changed in a digital age. Three television networks are not enough. One phone attached to a kitchen wall is not enough. A desktop computer alone is not enough. One home page for everything consumers need from a company or brand is not enough.

We expect everything to be tailored and expressive of who we are as individuals—not people tossed into one big group. This is why creating unique new name spaces will be so important. One home page won't be it—a neighborhood of domain names and pages for specific and unique needs across mobile, social, and online experiences will need to be created to meet the future demands of the consumer. This prediction follows the signals and trends. It creates the ability to zip-code the Internet into categories across digital experiences.

These new domain extensions, and particularly the new brand spaces, now operating at the root zone (or the very base) of the Internet are a natural evolution of what is happening in other facets of digital transformation. It's creating segmentation, categorization, and the ability to customize or make sense of a vast digital world. The Internet has just been broken into a few big categories, and the possibilities are endless.

In the boardroom, the big question should be, "Why will consumers care? Why will this impact our company?" Let's start with why consumers will care. This new, expanded space provides greater safety and security, is the next big thing, is easy to remember, and is custom and tailored—matching all the trends we've talked about.

**Security matters.** Greater security and trust are increasingly important in the digital world. I'll cover cybersecurity and what boards need to know about it in the next chapter, but, needless to say, we all are concerned about hacks, hijacking, phishing, or having our accounts or identity stolen. The new top-level domains give brands a chance to completely control their most important digital assets—their online presences.

Even mobile apps tie back to a web presence, so locking this down in a closed space your company can control simply makes sense. In the new Dot Brand space, brands can control each and every domain name issued in their spaces. So, they can promise to consumers that if it ends in dot-jpmorgan, dot-pnc, dot-amex, or dot-citi, to name just a few, then consumers can trust that the site is authentic and safe. At its most basic level, this is what consumers want from companies—some assurance that if they go somewhere online that it isn't a counterfeit or fraudulent site.

Take a look at these real search results for "American Express travel." After the sponsored ads, toward the bottom of the list, there are links that appear to be official American Express sites—but which ones are real and which ones are fake? It's hard to tell just by this list. When American Express can operate its own top-level domain, they can issue domain addresses to authorized travel partners only, offering greater assurances of trust and security to consumers.

And while phishing e-mails can't be completely stopped, these new secure spaces can create better visual indicators for consumers. For example, look at this real phishing e-mail I received.

Fig. 2.6. "American Express travel" search results

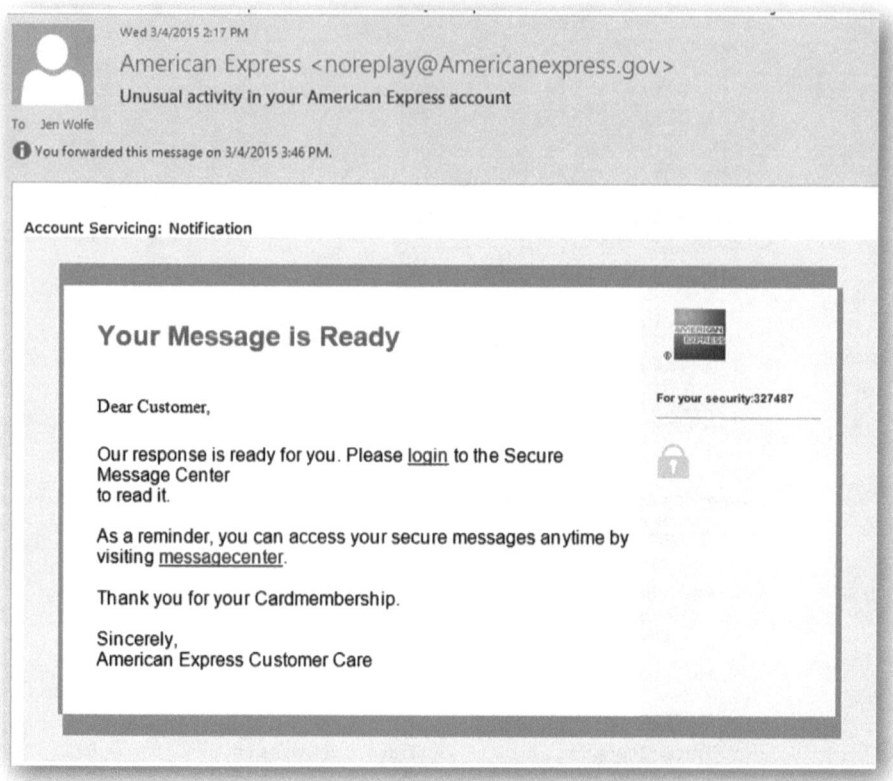

Fig. 2.7. American Express phishing e-mail

It looks like it's an official American Express e-mail. It has the logo, and it has an americanexpress.gov domain name. But there are a few indicators it's not real. First, the address says "noreplay" instead of "noreply." I doubt American Express is sending out e-mails with that obvious of a typo. And then there is something that looks like an account number, but it's not my account number. And, finally, the message itself seems off. *Our response is ready for you. Please login to the Secure Message Center to read it.* I hadn't contacted American Express, so why would their response be ready for me?

These were all immediate indicators that this was an e-mail intended to get me to log in and then have my credentials stolen. But a lot of people may not pick up on all of those signals, and in an instant, the bad guys have secure log-in information and can steal from the individual and from American Express.

## Digital in the Boardroom

By marketing to consumers to only trust a log in that ends in dot-amex or dot-americanexpress, American Express can ensure that consumers have some framework or visual indicator to know whether a domain address is issued by American Express.

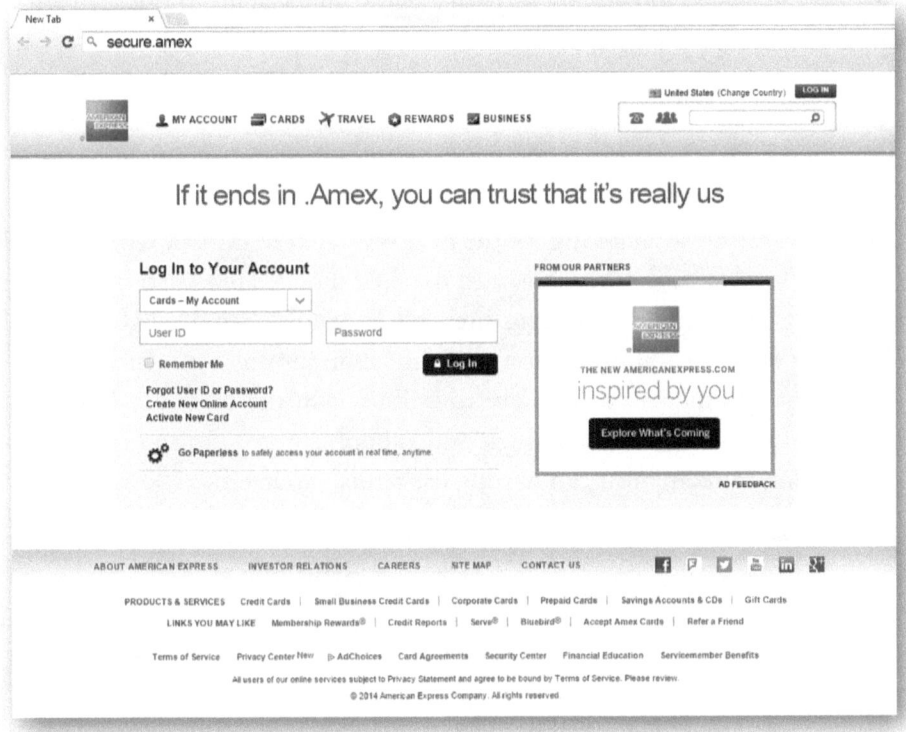

Fig. 2.8. Secure.amex

Some people may still fall prey to the scam, but it's one additional piece of protection that can stop unsuspecting consumers from clicking on a phishing link.

There will always be ways bad guys who try to work around and hack the system, but this provides an important, additional feature that never existed before. This is why the boardroom needs to understand what's at stake and ensure that status-quo thinking doesn't keep executives from considering future possibilities.

There are many more details of how layers of security can be added and how the Dot Brand can be used to build out internal systems and e-mail systems and create greater promises to consumers. But recognizing that this platform could create new security measures is what senior management needed to know during the application period, and that stemmed from ICANN policy. If they had stopped with a status-quo mentality, the CMO, CEO, and CIO might never have known anything about it, and the opportunity to solve this problem might have been missed.

Half the world's top brands, including many financial institutions, own such assets. The other half may apply for them in the future. What will your company do when faced with the opportunity to control your digital neighborhood?

### The Next Big Thing

Consumers are always looking for the next big thing in digital. Consider that in the last few years, they have flocked to using mobile apps or to sharing and connecting via social networking sites, all in your "digital neighborhood." These new spaces are about owning your most important asset. In a dot-com, you merely rent the space and have to build out in the same big channel as everyone else. Everyone from Google and Yahoo! to porn sites and counterfeiters are all in dot-com. You can hardly distinguish yourself.

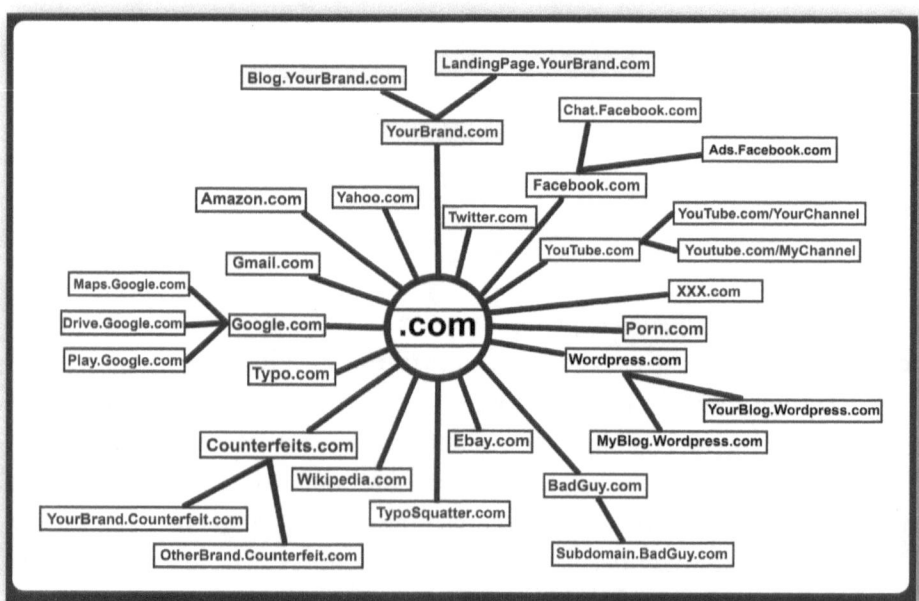

Fig. 2.9 The dot-com universe

## Digital in the Boardroom

In your own space, you completely own it, control it, and can design it to be what you want. Consider it your own parcel of digital real estate. This gives you the ability to create and design your own Internet neighborhood—the neighborhood you want. You design it to help people navigate the way you want them to rather than the way the dot-com spaces force you to. And you can track data in the space based on how consumers navigate, what they do, and where they go, but in a more targeted way because of the control you have over the space.

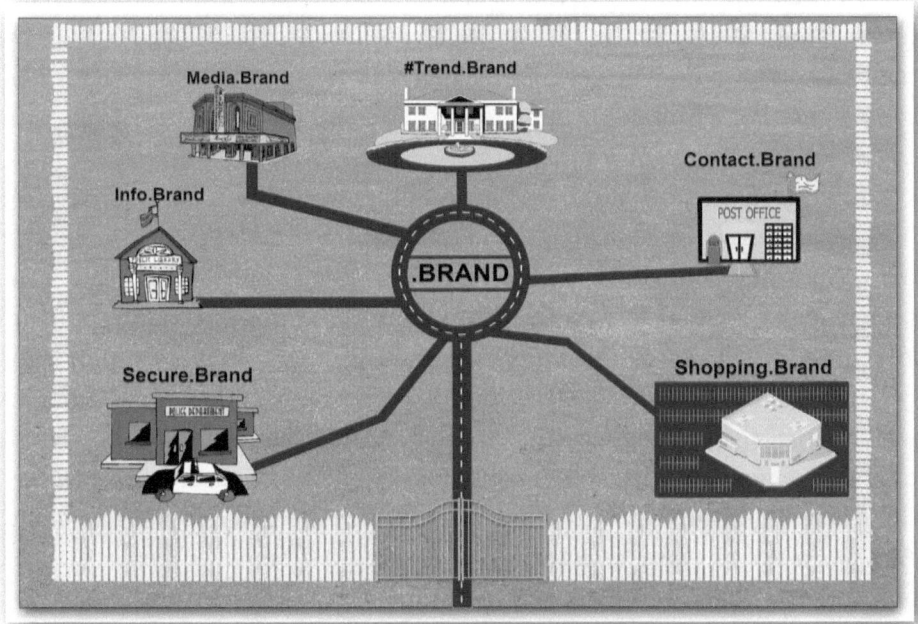

Fig. 2.10. A Dot-Brand neighborhood

This is an important distinction, because this control and ability to design the space means your company can not only create more security and authenticity and track new forms of data but can also create a better and more tailored user experience. Additionally, because you own the entire space, any new products you later invent or campaigns you create have places for them safely nested in your own Internet neighborhood. This gives your company the ability to respond to trends or even create trends. More important, it creates a catalyst for designing your entire digital experience in a new way.

Digital pay is showing up in Starbucks and other retailers, and Apple Pay wants to help you buy everything without pulling out your wallet. The Internet of things already exists, and consumer adoption is around the corner, connecting our refrigerators and thermostats to our televisions. Our things are now all minicomputers. In the online space, this creates the next big thing, and you can build it all in your exclusive digital neighborhood.

When consumers see new, hyper-niched, branded online places like run.nike or whathappensin.vegas, they will shift their behavior from blind searches into seeking out experiences they desire. Even outside of the Dot Brand spaces, the new top-level domains create the ability to form natural-language-based campaigns. For example, purposeful.life, grateful.life, alzheimers.solutions, cold.solutions, and freshfromthe.farm.

In these new spaces, if the Internet user types what he or she is looking for into the address bar and it matches an address, the browser takes you directly there. So, when companies market something that is more memorable, consumers may type that in directly, eliminating the concern that the company lose them in search results, which are often plagued with domain-investor gaming. When consumers see something memorable, they won't have to search for it; they will just go directly there. And even when they do search, or if they're not sure what they are looking for, early results already show that the search algorithms quickly come to recognize the new top-level domains. And when the top-level domain is that of a trusted brand, it means that the new spaces will get an organic search boost.

Fig. 2.11. RaysPizza.NYC

Fig. 2.12. WhatHappensIn.Vegas

Even nonprofits can build out bold statements in an easy-to-remember way. For example, Livestrong could build out howdoyou.livestrong. Beyond just these memorable statements, this new naming space allows brands to create custom and tailored spaces and messaging that is consistent with today's big-data trends. Rather than creating one domain-name space and building off of it, a brand can build a digital neighborhood that make sense, with individual addresses designed for targeted audiences, based upon the data they have available.

Consider a custom space like sally.closet.calvinklein. Calvin Klein can allow Sally, a consumer, to build her online closet and track not just her Calvin Klein purchases but her other purchases as well, giving Calvin Klein access to even more important data about her. They can use this data to drive design and purchase decisions and understand more about what she's buying across the landscape, not just in their neighborhood. Give consumers a way to build their wardrobes even outside your brand, and you know what they have in their closets.

Or consider joe.gifts.tiffany. Tiffany & Co. could more easily help Joe track all the gifts Joe buys and then make even better suggestions to him for future purchases around holidays and birthdays. Wouldn't that be valuable to companies who plan the next season and buy to meet consumer demands? All this data is available by creating the spaces consumers want and creating better experiences than currently exist. The Dot Brand space gives companies the ability to build digital neighborhoods in a more powerful and natural-language-based approach and to rethink the consumer experience in a newly evolved digital world.

Now that we can begin to see how mobile, social networking, digital payments, the Internet of things, and this new domain space can all work together, we can design a digital world to give consumers what they want and need rather than just apply new solutions to old problems.

## IF IT'S SO VALUABLE, WHY DOESN'T EVERYONE DO IT?

You may now be wondering if your company has a Dot Brand, and, if so, what it is doing with it. And if your company doesn't own one, you may be questioning why it doesn't. The reality is that in 2012, when this opportunity presented itself, the only people who really knew anything about it were trademark lawyers. And the trademark lawyers were being briefed by brand-protection companies, many of whom had a reputation for aggressive, fear-based sales tactics. At the time, trademark lawyers desperately tried to engage marketing or digital leaders inside companies, but without the information we have today, those leaders had little interest in disruptive thinking. The messaging that sold most trademark lawyers on the idea was about the fear of someone else getting a company's Dot Brand space rather than about the advantages of all of these innovative new benefits.

This fear, however, reinforced the status-quo culture, which was enough to ensure that in most companies, not a lot of attention was paid to this quiet Internet revolution. Instead, the lawyers focused on a defensive strategy, with a mentality of "buy it just in case someday the marketing people want to use it sometime in the future." As new, big generic spaces came on board, not a lot of money was pumped into advertising. The result is that most people remain largely unaware that the makings of a paradigm shift are already underway.

In most instances when I briefed key executives at Fortune 100 companies on this idea, I was met with resistance and the status-quo thinking that dot-com would always be the only thing anyone needed on the Internet. What do *you* think? Can we really believe that the Internet is never going to grow, evolve, or change? This is why I began this chapter by outlining other big paradigm shifts and how this one fits into a repeating pattern. When we talk about the future, it's about understanding the signals. Many signals indicate that a massive digital transformation of our society and business is underway. The quiet revolution of the Internet is one important signal to understanding the future of the digital world. Every company is digital, and this is one big piece of the digital puzzle.

Consider the Digital Map I mentioned. As you go around your digital world and map your space, ask what online experience your company provides. Does your company make it easy for consumers to move from one digital platform to the next? Do you create a seamless experience no matter where the consumers are, and do you fully understand what they want and need before they do? What works, and what doesn't? How do consumers navigate in and out of your digital spaces? What is the experience, and how can you improve it? By understanding how your customers move in and out of your spaces and how they intersect between their real and digital worlds, as I described in chapter 1, you can begin to see where the future of digital needs to be for your company. Domain names are one piece of it.

What's most interesting is that once some of the big technology companies realized what Google and Amazon had, they wanted in. During the ICANN meeting in October of 2015 in Dublin, Twitter executive Steve Coates said the following:

> I would like to make a suggestion that we work on a parallel path going into round two [i.e., ICANN's opening of a second round of applications so that more companies may apply for top-level domains] and also suggest perhaps an expedited process for dot brands. So moving forward with a single registrant closed dot brands…will allow us applicants who are not—who did not participate or were not around during round one—to take advantage of some of the security benefits that operating a top-level domain have, as well as some of the DNS innovations that can be explored in that process, which I think will help ensure success of the TLD program. *For more information, go to ICANN.org for the public transcript from the ICANN 54 Meeting in Dublin during the Public Forum.*

Citing the security benefits as a primary reason for its interest in a Dot Brand, clearly Twitter has recognized that it missed the boat in failing to apply back in 2012, further reinforcing the value of Dot Brands. I'll continue to cite throughout the book as we cover the digital map how these new Dot Brands can integrate into a future digital strategy. One additional point to the expansion of top-level domains: for the first time in the history of the Internet, internationalized domain names were offered—in other words, the actual characters in Chinese, Japanese, Korean, Arabic, or Cyrillic were available in domain names. For businesses operating in these markets, the impact could be transformative for companies that are prepared to meet the expectations of consumers better than those without digital addresses in their native languages.

Now that I've covered the big signals of change and how to be prepared for the big change occurring in the Internet, it's time to dig into cybersecurity.

## KEY TAKEAWAYS FROM CHAPTER 2

* New top-level domains will categorize and segment the Internet by big brands and by interest, creating the "zip codes" of the Internet. This is a completely new paradigm, marking the beginning of the next generation of the Internet.
* Google, Amazon, and half the world's top brands will transform the way consumers come to understand the domain name as a signal of authentication and credibility, moving consumers toward more natural-language-based identification of digital addresses across the Internet landscape.
* Companies operating the Dot Brand will leverage better strategies for data, search, security, consumer engagement online, and control of their most important digital asset. The Dot Brand is the backbone for all things digital.

You need to be aware of these coming changes and ensure your company is paying attention to the signals of change so that you are ready and armed with the assets you need.

*Chapter 3*

# THE CYBERSECURITY THREAT

In June 2013, I attended the Stanford Law School Director's College executive program. Most of the attendees are longtime board members of publicly traded companies. At the program, "Cybersecurity" was a plenary session that packed the house with standing room only. A panel of experts apprised the audience of directors that the number-one risk every company faced was a cyberattack. Representatives from the US government warned that the threat was far greater than most senior management members understood and that the immanency of corporate attacks was all but certain.

Mary E. Galligan, a retired special agent from the FBI in Cyber/Special Operations, had particularly chilling remarks about the reality that most companies had already been attacked in small ways and that future big attacks were a certainty. The silence that filled the room was deafening. This powerful roomful of people knew that the risk of cyberattack was all too real, but uncertain of how to solve such an enormous problem, even in the heart of Silicon Valley. In the months and years that followed that presentation, we have seen several major attacks on US corporations: Home Depot, Target, Anthem, Sony, and then, embarrassingly, Ashley Madison (the infamous dating website for people who seek extramarital affairs). Even the US Office of Personnel Management was attacked. And these are just the ones that made headlines. Consider the thousands of other smaller businesses facing attacks that are never reported in the mainstream news.

One of the most scandalous of these big attacks came in December 2014, when the board of directors of Sony awoke to learn that private and personal e-mails, including confidential and embarrassing personal information of celebrities, key executives, and thousands of employees, had been hacked and made public on the deep web. *PC Magazine* defines the "deep web" as a set of clandestine websites that are hidden from the public—this is web content that cannot be found on Google, Yahoo!, or Bing searches because it has been coded not to be indexed by search engines or is only available to users when they are on a particular site. The deep web is thousands of times larger than the public web (also referred to as the surface web).

Despite earlier attacks on companies like Target, Home Depot, and Anthem since Mary Galligan's warning at Stanford in 2013, this one stood out for many because it was not for the obvious financial reasons as were the others. The other attacks had targeted consumer credit cards or identity information for the financial gain of the hackers and their buyers.

The attack on Sony was done for political reasons, purportedly as a vendetta against the company releasing the film *The Interview*. It was a wake-up call for CEOs and their boards across the planet. Not only was every company vulnerable, but its very commercial activity, if it displeased someone with the means to wreak havoc, could prompt an attack. What was even more startling was the realization that these kinds of attacks have been happening for several years. (I've provided a list of cybersecurity breaches affecting public companies at the end of this chapter.)

Cybersecurity-risk experts recognize, of course, that some companies are at greater risk than others. Energy companies, for example, could be targeted for political reasons with terrorist or hostile activities that try to hurt people or disrupt everyday life. And financial institutions are at risk of economic espionage for financial gain. Companies like Sony with high-profile media messages can also be at risk if they disseminate political or social views that provoke groups with the means and desire to cause harm.

The last few years have brought this issue to the forefront of boardrooms. In the boardroom, you don't have to understand the details of how cyberattackers do what they do, but you do need to know how it can be managed and mitigated and how it fits into a larger digital strategy for the company. This book is about digital in the boardroom, and cybersecurity and digital will always overlap in some way. Surveys provided to the National Association of Corporate Directors have shown that most boards relegate the management of cybersecurity to the audit committee. According to the *Governance of Cybersecurity: 2015 Report*, a global study developed by the Georgia Tech Information Security Center, cybersecurity has risen to become one of the top boardroom issues, with nearly two-thirds of survey respondents actively addressing computer and information security, up from 33 percent in 2012. Most boards have established risk committees separate from audit committees. PwC's annual Corporate Director Survey found similar results, with concerns about cybersecurity up nearly 30 percent from the prior year. PwC's study also found that this is one of the greatest areas where boards want to spend more time.

But, like all facets of digital, cybersecurity can no longer operate in a silo in one sector of the company or as one piece of an already-overwhelming job just for the audit committee. Senior management and the board cannot simply assume that someone in IT or legal is taking care of it. Much like finance requires independent audits, cybersecurity, too, may soon require independent oversight by the Securities and Exchange Commission. This paramount issue requires oversight and assurance that a company has checks and balances in place to minimize the threat. I use the word *minimize*, and not *eliminate*, intentionally. You cannot eliminate this threat. You can, however, mitigate it by understanding how it intersects with all facets of your digital operations and integrate its management as part of your strategy.

The primary reason for this is that everything your company does in the digital world can be a metaphorical door or window left open for the bad guys to break into your digital house. Marketing departments are notorious for building apps or creating new websites without cross-checking with IT. Additionally, everything people representing your company do and say in a vast digital world could now prompt a response in social media that spans the globe in a matter of minutes. Digital messages can turn something meant to be clever, funny, or as a response to a trend into a geopolitical or social provocation for a cyberattack. This is far beyond just social-media training for your sales reps; it's about fundamentally understanding interconnectivity at all levels and setting company policies and management structures in place to mitigate these increasingly likely risks to your firm.

Today, your company engages other companies, vendors, consumers, and users in a digital world in many ways:

1. Traditional online websites, including microsites and niched places across thousands of digital addresses (Ask your Webmaster how many pages you have out there—it's probably thousands or possibly millions, depending upon the size of your company.)
2. Mobile applications and engagements
3. Social networking
4. E-commerce platforms
5. Cloud-based computing with vendors and customers, as well as on the internal network
6. The Internet of things: televisions, thermostats, refrigerators, cars, watches, eyeglasses (Everything will soon be connected, and your digital world will interact at many points. Even the security system at your physical place of business is connected to the Internet.)
7. E-mails and other forms of one-on-one communication, all of which can become the source for one click to launch an attack into your systems

In every one of these digital spaces, someone could leave an opening for a hacker to get into your systems and spread damage virally to accomplish his or her goal—to steal from you, shut you down, punish you, blackmail you, or simply embarrass you.

Additionally, every one of these platforms can be a space where a misplaced message can give rise to a spark that initiates hatred or greed to attack you. It doesn't really matter what your business is about; the risk is there for every company, and now it's a matter of managing it. Remember the dentist who shot the beloved lion in Africa? Social media gave the world a platform to launch hate attacks on the Minnesota dentist.

Digital in the Boardroom

But why should you concern yourself with this at the board level? Shouldn't this be something your information-technology department is handling? This is a common misconception. For decades now, everything tech related has been handed over to information technology to handle, as you might imagine. But there is too much integration across marketing, legal, and this newly forming digital category for this to be an effective strategy. As a board, you can't get into the weeds of solving the problems, but you are responsible for oversight, which means you need a holistic approach to preparing for trouble beyond just pushing it to IT.

Much like the audit committee functions to ensure the financial health of the company and that checks and balances are in order to meet regulatory requirements, a cybersecurity and digital committee is necessary to ensure a company's cybersecurity and digital health is in order. In many instances, however, these functions are still in a silo rather than managed as a cohesive strategy.

In this chapter, I've highlighted a few of the big questions board members should ask and a checklist for next steps. Above all, boards should now consider a separate committee to focus on oversight of the company's cybersecurity and digital programs.

## YOUR DIGITAL ECOSYSTEM

Your digital ecosystem is about more than just your computer systems, e-mail, or electronic files. The digital world has become so vast it has enveloped most facets of your organization. But there are some records that are particularly vulnerable. In chapter 1, I recommended that you conduct an exercise I refer to as Digital Mapping®, where you actually map out your digital world. When your team conducts this exercise, it's helpful to identify those records or digital assets that could be at greatest risk if compromised as part of the process.

Consider your sensitive data segments:

**Data protected by privacy laws.** Increasingly, around the planet, what is defined as personal or private, protectable data is identified as protected or held to a heightened standard. If you are compromised on data protected by privacy laws, the cost to your company can be more than just a quarterly earnings dip; it can be a deep hole to dig out of over years, not months.

In some jurisdictions, there are penalties and fines for such breaches, creating even further costs. Think insurance will cover it all? Ask Target about that one. They've struggled to recover in public perception after the breach. If someone wants to attack you, the threat of releasing data protected by privacy laws could hold your management team hostage to the potential costs.

What is the gate that secures this information? Are there extra checks to ensure that only appropriate information is released? Mapping how sensitive information is accessed and maintained is just the starting point. Such information includes **health records,** which are typically expected to be given a higher level of protection, even a level above privacy laws; and **financial records**, which can include everything from consumer credit cards or account numbers to your company's confidential financial information.

**E-mail.** While we all know we need to be careful what we put into e-mail, the reality is that most people, even senior management, often treat e-mail like an assumed confidential conversation, quipping back and forth with like-minded colleagues. But when e-mail gets hacked, everything you wrote in it may be available for public scrutiny, not to mention the fact that even encrypted e-mails can be vulnerable to unwanted eavesdroppers. Consider former secretary of state Hillary Clinton and the e-mail scandal that rocked her seemingly unchallenged Democratic bid for the White House. Every e-mail you write can be subject to scrutiny.

**Intellectual Property.** Patents, trade secrets, copyrights, trademarks, domain names, and your business strategy and plans are all stored in documents across your digital landscape. If a hacker gets his or her hands on enough confidential or nonpublic information, he or she can do some real harm. In some instances, hackers want your intellectual property so that some entity can compete with you.

According to Eric Schmidt, "In late 2009, Google detected unusual traffic within its network and began to monitor activity. What was discovered was a highly sophisticated industrial attack on Google's intellectual property coming from China." In the end, this attack—which targeted not only Google but also dozens of other publicly listed companies—was among the driving factors in Google's decision to alter its business position in China, resulting in the shutdown of Google China operations.

**Algorithms and secure-authentication procedures.** Even algorithms you have built or are working on could be hacked and compromised. Most companies run their own algorithms somewhere in their digital ecosystems. You also likely have documentation describing secure-authentication procedures. In the wrong hands, it's like giving away the key to your digital house.

**All that customer data.** Your company is likely tracking and aggregating a lot of data to draw important market conclusions and drive customer behavior. This could become a target if you have become particularly good at data collection. For example, companies like Google, Facebook, and Amazon possess an unfathomable amount of data on each of us. It's not just our credit-card numbers or financial information, but personal information such what movies and books we like, what we buy and when we buy it, how we communicate with others socially, and on and on. Their vast profiling of all of us into advertising categories could have disastrous impacts if used for nefarious purposes.

**High-profile, confidential information.** Your human-resources department is likely storing private, health, personal, and compensation-related information about every employee in your company. If your company includes any high-profile individuals, like Sony does, accessing that information could be highly lucrative to a would-be blackmailer.

**Social media.** Don't forget all the social-media information on all of your senior management and board members, in particular, but also employees throughout the company. Someone with bad motives could profile your senior manager's use of Facebook, Twitter, Instagram, and other social media to gather information about his or her life and blackmail your company with it.

Here's one example of a vulnerability: most people post pictures of their vacations on these social media channels—it's a great way to clue in potential burglars of their homes and a great way to let hackers know when senior managers or key security personnel are out of the office. Even the simple act of posting family photos over the holidays, if done by enough key personnel, can clue hackers in to a weak point back at the office—the A team is all on vacation.

Key personnel or senior managers should be trained to limit what they post on social media with respect to potential exposure of the company to threats. It's important that your senior managers, board members, and employees with access to sensitive information not list their places of employment in any publicly accessible social-media feeds.

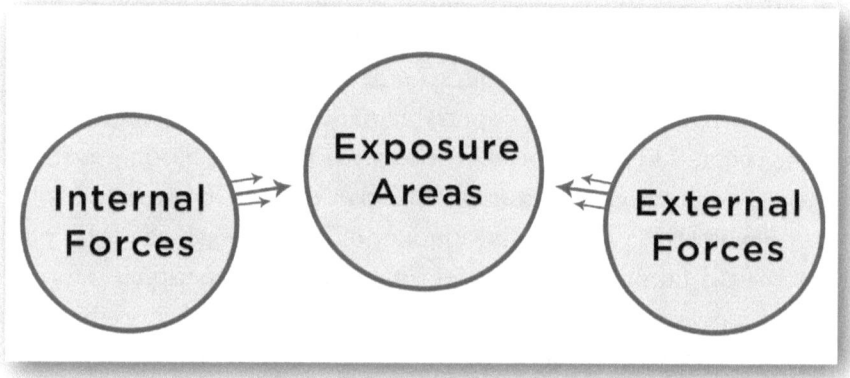

Fig. 3.1. Security-impact zones

## EXPOSURE POINTS

Let's take a look at your company's exposure points. They include internal and external factors as well as reasons you could be targeted.

### Internal Factors

Internal factors are where you presumably have the most control. These include the following:

> **Internal system weaknesses.** Any weaknesses or gaps in security in your internal network are the first things to consider. Entire books exist on architecting secure internal networks and systems. A brief Amazon search delivers more than a thousand titles dealing with cybersecurity. Your IT department is familiar with these books and

strategies. While you don't need to know the details, you do need to understand how this fits into the security matrix.

**Passwords and credentials.** How passwords are managed and how frequently they are changed are also critical to minimizing exposure points. Ever watch spy movies and see how they break into establishments? They almost always impersonate someone using his or her credentials. Does life imitate art, or does art imitate life? Managing passwords and credentials well is essential. In a *Wall Street Journal* article, Punam Keller asserts that most people still do not select secure passwords, so ensuring that passwords are as secure as possible and changed regularly is a painful but important checkpoint.

**Employee devices and personal digital.** Your weakest link could potentially be your own employees. When they use personal devices or log in to their personal social-media or other accounts from work, this creates holes and potential ways in for someone with bad intentions. Particularly, as you consider the vast number of employees across the organization, you'll see how many holes there are. Some workers may be loyal and never do anything compromising intentionally, but some may naively allow access or download something that looks innocent but contains a hidden threat. They might respond to phishing e-mails and personal banking information. However, some employees may not be loyal; or, they may be careless or even reckless.

**Senior-management and board-member devices and personal digital.** Senior management is likely a bit more diligent than others in the organization, but even savvy and sophisticated managers can make mistakes when accessing personal information or using devices, assuming they're safe. Cracking down on use of personal devices and access to personal digital properties could help minimize exposure points. Likewise, board members insisting on using their own tablets or laptops could unwittingly be creating exposure points in how sensitive information is transmitted.

**Internal use of the cloud.** Of course, cloud computing is a critical issue, one that every company now faces. All vendors use some form of the cloud, and most won't indemnify beyond the value of the contract. Managing cloud risks is increasingly important, particularly ensuring that employees are not using their own personal cloud accounts to transfer documents or information.

**Wi-Fi for guests.** Most companies provide Wi-Fi for guests. Are the username and password changed regularly? For vendors who visit regularly, their devices may simply remember the Wi-Fi username and password. If one of these devices were stolen, would it create an opening? Presumably, guest Wi-Fi is limited, but once someone breaches one barrier, another will likely follow.

**Physical premises.** Finally, the physical premises are also important in managing security in general, but certainly from preventing a cybersecurity attack. How easily can someone access your building and then stick a flash drive into a computer somewhere?

### External Factors

Numerous external factors impact your ability to stay one step ahead of cybersecurity in your digital world:

**Nontech Vendors.** Your vendors interact with your digital world daily. When and how do they engage and interact with you? How are files shared and distributed? In the Target hack, the hackers used stolen vendor credentials, which means that for many companies, it's not just the cybersecurity program you need to worry about; it's your vendors' programs as well. A vendor that seemingly has no connection to the technology you use can leave open a hole. Every vendor, no matter how large or small, is a potential source of an issue. How many employees in your company can subscribe to a website or a file-sharing server or buy something online with a corporate credit card, engaging yet another vendor?

Each of these interactions increases the potential for not just waste and duplication of services but also for unlocking information unknowingly. In Target's case, it didn't separate its sensitive data from networks that a vendor working on the HVAC, for instance, might access.

**Start-up technologies.** One of the biggest challenges companies face in the digital world is responding to the next big thing, the latest new technology created by some start-up somewhere in the world that takes off and then becomes part of their digital strategy. We never know where the next one will come from. Foursquare uses geolocation tracking on devices, as do most other apps. Tinder knows what kind of person you find attractive, as do many others. These new technologies are gaining private and personal information tied to your devices at an increasingly rapid pace.

**Social media.** Your company is undoubtedly engaging on social media. You may have a corporate presence on Facebook and Twitter, but what about the hundreds of other social-media sites? Where do you have your official pages? Who controls and manages those assets? Is it an internal employee or someone external? Is someone considering the threats posed in cybersecurity when your company (or its representative) interacts and responds? And how do your employees represent themselves in social media? Do they list where they work? If so, can you control what they say?

**Cloud and tech vendors.** The cloud is now a way of life for consumers. Everyone stores their music, videos, photos, documents, and whatever else they want in a cloud so that everything is convenient to access from a variety of devices, and they can upgrade devices as desired without losing any data. For companies, cloud-based services are quickly becoming the only way to do business. Many feel safety in numbers here. If your Microsoft cloud goes down or gets hacked, then presumably, everyone using the Microsoft cloud is in the same boat. But at some point, that may no longer be good enough. Your company's cloud usage needs a deep-dive analysis to find the weaknesses and opportunities for someone who wants to do you harm.

**The Internet of things.** How is your company engaging with the Internet of things? Most people now have televisions hanging on their walls or gaming systems connected to the Internet. Some may have thermostats or security systems at home that connect to the Internet, and the security system in your building probably does too. A few early adopters might have refrigerators or cars that do this. Soon, smart homes and cars will be as common as smartphones. As this happens, your company will undoubtedly engage with all of these things. Where does it do so now, and where are the exposure points?

**Mobile and apps.** Likewise, mobile devices are currently used to access your digital world. Are you tracking that access, and what do you do with that data?

**Big tech drivers.** Last, big tech drivers will continue to push and change the digital experience. Our privacy will continue to erode in favor of convenience and algorithms that can deliver what we want to our homes at the moment our brains realize we want it. Just look at the patents being filed by Google, Amazon, Facebook, Intel, Adobe, and many others, and you can see the future of digital. For example, Google has filed patents for everything from verifying human use to protecting a browser (like Chrome) from piracy. Or, Amazon is working on detecting network attacks and techniques to protect against denial-of-service attacks. Apple has a long list of patents that focus on authentication and security, as do companies like Disney, eBay, Intel, and Verizon, to name just a few. Studying this information can help us determine how cybersecurity is being addressed by the big concerns and what your company should be doing. From a cybersecurity perspective, the erosion of privacy in addition to the interconnectivity of devices in and out of our personal and work lives means more exposure points and opportunities for those who wish to harm us.

All of these internal and external sources track data and information, which creates openings, weaknesses, and more possibilities for attack through your own, your employees', and your vendors' digital activity.

## EXPOSURE AREAS CYBERSECURITY QUIZ

It's important to assess your threat points as an organization. Answer these questions to begin finding exposure points you might have. Each yes counts as one point.

**Financial Exposure**

* Do you store or process consumers' credit-card or financial information?
* Are you a bank or financial institution?
* Do you allow bitcoin transactions?
* Are employees provided corporate credit cards and allowed to set their own usernames and passwords on financial accounts?

**Messaging Exposure**

* Do your senior managers manage their own social-media accounts (such as Twitter or Facebook) and have their positions with your company publicly listed there?
* Does your company put out content—videos, articles, movies, or any other media form—that comments on social or political issues of the day?
* Do you do business in Russia, Brazil, India, or China?
* Do you do business in hostile areas controlled by governments that do not value free speech or are run by dictators or violent leaders driven by geopolitical or religious fanatics?
* Are you subject to activist investors?

**Blackmail Exposure**

* Do you maintain sensitive information such as health-care records?
* Do you have access to information about high-profile people?

* Do you have access to sensitive information (like Ashley Madison did) or just personal information, like behavior on social networks?
* Do you maintain intellectual property or trade secrets to cutting-edge technologies?
* Do you maintain intellectual property for weapons that could be used for terrorist activities?
* Do you have any disgruntled terminated employees, contractors, or vendors? Are you sure?

**Disruption Exposure**

* Do you manage functions critical to our society, such as energy, power, transportation, phones, communication, television, provide internet services or news and information to the masses?
* Do you operate a school or health-care institution?
* Do you provide support to government operations?
* Do you operate satellites?
* Do you provide a service some feel is offensive or immoral?

Did you end up with a score of four points or more? If so, you are at risk. Do you have a cybersecurity-risk-mitigation plan? What will you do if you are attacked? How are you managing corporate communications, including social media, to mitigate risk exposure? How will you respond if someone tries to blackmail you? No one wants to be held hostage, but understanding your threat points can help you prepare your leadership for it before it happens. What will you do if your systems go down?

According to NetSecurity.org, 95 percent of all attacks are financially motivated. While many think small companies are less at risk, the reality is that hackers may view smaller companies that serve bigger companies as a means to an end—get the small fish, and then get to the bigger one. But attacks on Ashley Madison suggest that there could be an increasing number of blackmail-driven attacks. Ashley Madison was threatened to close the service

Digital in the Boardroom

down or else face the public humiliation of its members. The company, about to enter into an IPO, did not close the service, and its members' names were released. In any case, of course, the big targets are being hit steadily.

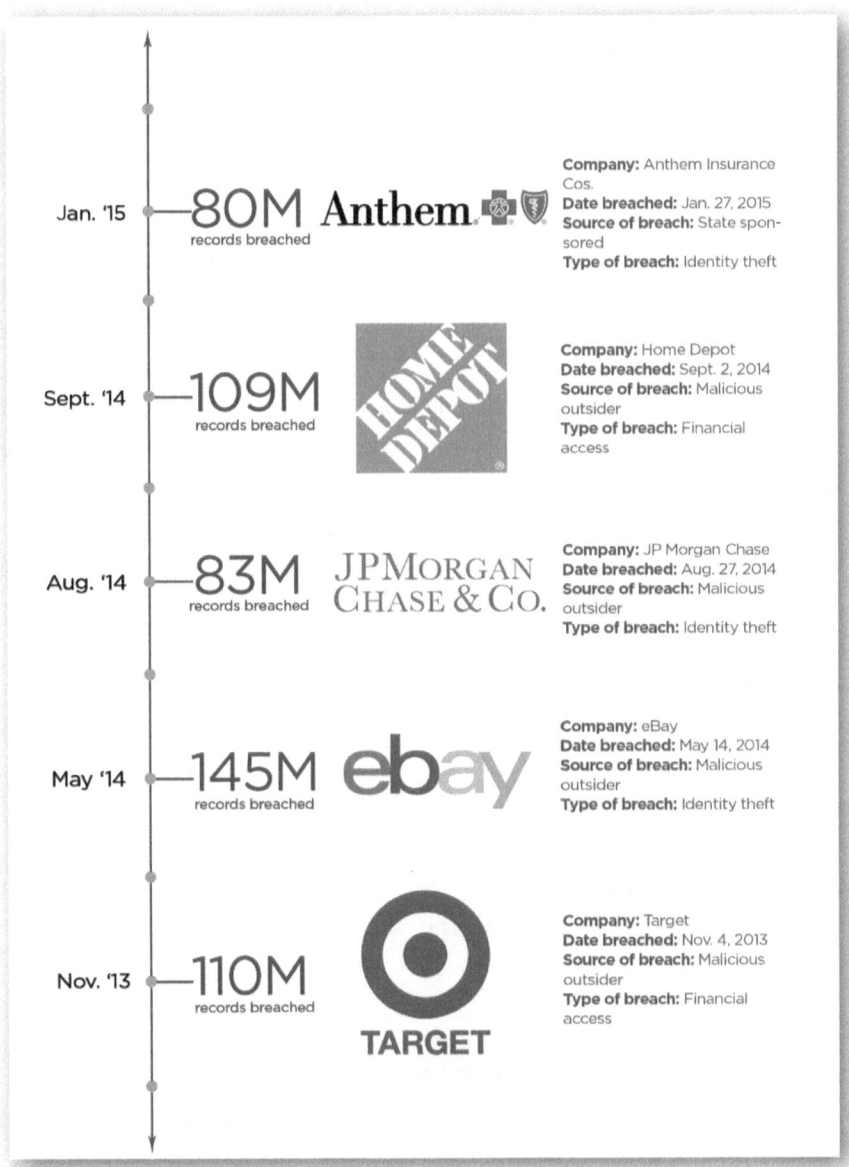

Fig. 3.2. Big security breaches by the numbers

These threats can come in many forms. Even a fraudulent domain name can create confusion. Twitter has faced several potential hacks:

* After the *New York Post*'s Twitter account posted bogus news about US interest-rate policy and China firing missiles on a US Navy ship, the newspaper confirmed that the account had been hacked.
* Hackers hijacked the *Associated Press*'s Twitter account, sending stock markets down 1 percent in seconds by posting a false claim of an attack on the White House.
* When a fake domain name appearing to be a Bloomberg news site reported that Twitter was going to be acquired for $31 billion, the social-media company's share price jumped 8 percent.

These are just a couple of examples of how social media can be hijacked and how quickly the market responds. And increasingly, CEOs are being held accountable for these breaches. Target's CEO, a thirty-five-year employee, resigned after forty million customers had their credit-card numbers stolen during the holiday season. According to a *Forbes* magazine article, the Target board of directors was also under significant pressure, and activist investors recommended that seven directors be kicked out, citing that the board had failed to protect the company from the breach and that it was their responsibility in oversight.

Boards are the checks and balances of their organization, responsible for oversight to protect investors. With the looming threat of not just *if* an attack happens, but *when*, preparing for it is part of the board's role. Even the US government takes this seriously. A *Wall Street Journal* article asserts that countries are amassing digital weapons and reconfiguring their militaries to prepare for cyber war.

## EMPLOYEES, VENDORS, CONTRACTORS...EVEN CUSTOMERS
Everyone you transact with can be a weak link in your chain. Employees, contractors, or even vendors who become disgruntled with company

## Digital in the Boardroom

policies, the nature of the business, or the way they are treated can become points of vulnerability. Edward Snowden, one of the most famous government contractors, compromised the National Security Agency from the inside, with full access granted to him. Because he decided—on his own, without any authority—that he didn't agree with the current policy, he chose to release that information to the world. What if one of your contractors with access to the most confidential and proprietary information of your company decides that he or she doesn't like how you do business and thinks the world should know? The list of possible complaints from disgruntled contractors are endless. Walmart has been accused of not paying benefits; Apple of hoarding money offshore. Retailers are often accused of using cheap labor in unsafe conditions. If you have been a target of complaints about how you do business in the past, it could resurface in a cyberattack from the inside.

Beyond even such a malicious act, employees, contractors, and vendors with direct access to your systems need to be trained on how to identify and handle phishing e-mails or phone calls looking for proprietary information. All it takes is one employee logged into your system and linking to a menu from a fraudulent e-mail that looks like it's from a local restaurant or trying to access a phishing site that is well disguised as his or her local bank—and the bad guys are in.

They also need to be trained on an evolving digital space and how they create vulnerabilities for themselves. Many social-media aficionados post on Facebook about where they are and live tweet, minute by minute, what they are doing. Train your teams how to avoid being targets—for themselves and for your company.

Your managers need to pay attention to employees and contractors with access to confidential information. Did Edward Snowden give away any signs of his political beliefs or motivations? The *Guardian* published a detailed chronicle of Snowden's life and what led him to be the biggest whistleblower of our time—it sheds light on the signs managers might have seen. At first, he was very outwardly against whistleblowers, despite what ultimately happened. His political rhetoric in insider chat rooms suggested a growing anger. Despite a rather sketchy résumé—being discharged early from the military and having no college degree—he worked his way up in government IT positions, saying specifically, "The degree thing is crap, at least domestically. If you really have ten years of solid provable IT experience, you can get a very well-paying IT job," in a statement online in July 2006.

By 2013, Snowden had landed a job with private contractor Booz Allen Hamilton, giving him access to the information he would later leak. If Booz Allen Hamilton, noted as one of the most prominent consulting companies in the world, could miss the signs, do you think your company might, too?

Political beliefs against the company or organization for which an employee works are nothing new. And even seemingly benign companies often face political questions. Many companies like Gap, H&M, Zara, and even Apple have been targeted for using cheap labor and human-rights violations to make more money. If an employee suddenly decides that something is not right and believes it so powerfully that he or she is willing to risk criminal sanctions, like Edward Snowden did, that employee can become a potential threat.

### The Cost to Your Organization and How to Prepare

What happens if you are attacked? While you can insure some of it, insurance typically doesn't cover the entire exposure. And keep in mind that if a small vendor is indemnifying you from this type of loss, it probably won't still be in business if it happens. So, yes, you can insure it up to a point. You can try to transfer liability to another party. But after that, you have to mitigate the risk through your operational effectiveness.

Projections of future losses from cybersecurity are estimated to be between $9 and $21 trillion in global economic-value creation. Since its 2013 data theft, Target has been fighting to regain customer confidence. The cumulative expenses related to the breach reached $236 million, offset

## Digital in the Boardroom

by $90 million in insurance. At least three thousand US companies were the victims of cybersecurity attacks in 2014, with a combined estimated cost of $400 billion.

All too often, cybersecurity-risk management is viewed as an expense instead of an investment. The cost of not being prepared could be devastating, particularly for smaller or tech- and IP-driven start-up companies where boards serve as oversight for rapidly growing management teams.

The types of losses you can incur can interrupt your business and damage your reputation. A very common form of attack that nearly every business faces is a denial-of-service attack. Also commonly referred to as D-DOS, this attack means that your digital properties are down until the hack is corrected. Customer support, e-commerce activities, and lost revenue are just a few of the potential costs to a business, not to mention losing the reputation of being a safe or secure company.

In the digital age, cybersecurity should be part of the overall digital strategy. With a holistic approach, the key is to audit, prepare, and practice. It's easy to put cybersecurity off in an IT bucket and tell the department to make sure problems don't happen. The IT people will do the best they can, but in today's digital world, the reality is that what your company does in other facets of digital (i.e., mobile, social, online, and e-commerce) can open the door to cyberattacks in more and more new ways. To be prepared, you must have your cybersecurity and digital operations work in close connection to understand exposure points, and you must have plans. How do you prepare?

### Audit, Prepare, Practice

1. Audit your organization for internal and external exposure points. Understand your entire digital ecosystem, and prepare a map of exposure points, building a Cyber dashboard like the one in Figure 3.3.

2. Develop a response plan and strategy, including potentially lost communications, to ensure your organization is prepared to continue to operate in a state of emergency.
    a. What is the board's protocol in a cybersecurity emergency? How will you communicate and connect—and what do you do if e-mail isn't working?
    b. What is senior leadership's response?
3. How are employees using personal devices and social media? Audit and develop policies to minimize exposures. Train senior managers how to manage social media in the digital age of cybersecurity threats (see below).
4. Based upon your audit, create a dashboard where you can score and track your company's readiness to address cybersecurity threats.
5. Practice and drill yourself to be sure you're ready if a cybersecurity attack occurs.
6. Repeat the process. You're never "done" here. The ways that bad guys attack change every day. Remember *The Imitation Game*—the movie about how the Nazis changed communication codes each and every day during WWII? It's a perfect analogy. Those who wish to do you harm will change their codes constantly. Your employees will continue to change, and new social-media and digital technologies will emerge. This issue never goes away. It's like accounting: as long as you are in business, everything has to be accounted for and reported.

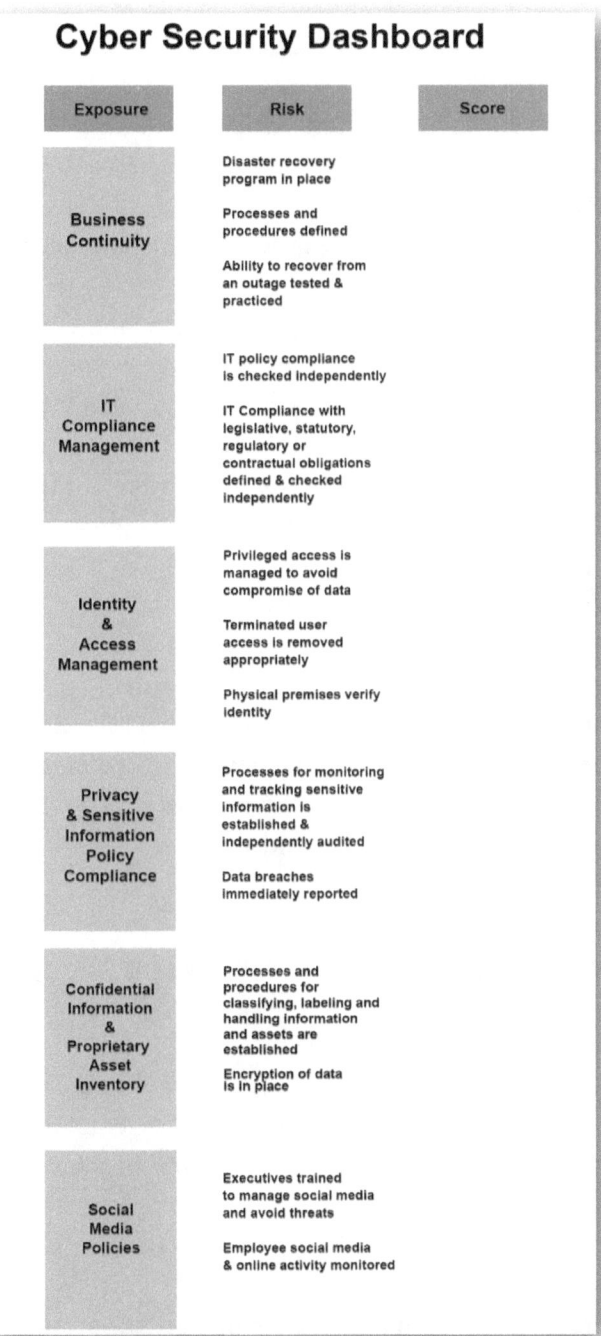

Fig. 3.3. Cybersecurity dashboard

Key Questions to Consider on All of Your Data-Exposure Points

1. Have we identified our most critical assets that we cannot afford to lose and/or systems for handling unplanned outages? What are our digital crown jewels?
2. Have we assessed the data exposure points and believe our assets are secure?
3. Who has access to our digital information, and how?
4. How are all the access points and exposure points managed?
5. How do vendors access data about our company? How do they store our company data on their own systems?
6. What cloud-based services do we use to store our information?
7. How are passwords assigned and changed regularly?
8. Can flash drives be used?
9. What happens if we are blackmailed?
10. What happens if we are attacked—how do we convene to make immediate decisions and minimize exposure?
11. What insurance do we have in place? What can and can't it do for us?
12. What zero-tolerance policy do we need in the organization for security breaches or lapses in security measures?
13. Who would likely attack us, and why?
14. Where are our biggest vulnerabilities?
15. Are we running drills?
16. Have we been informed on prior attacks and how severe they were?
17. How will we know if we have been hacked or breached?
18. Who are our likely adversaries?
19. If someone wanted to damage us, how could they hurt us the most?
20. How are security clearances provided to employees? What about guests? Are they checked periodically and benchmarked against performance reviews?
21. Do we monitor social-media or online posts of employees with critical access to information?
22. Where do senior management, legal, marketing, and the IT team differ on how they handle digital information? (This could be one of

the most important and yet difficult pieces of information to get for oversight.)
23. Do our vendors have clear cybersecurity measures in place? Do we monitor those measures?
24. How are we addressing the security vulnerabilities of a mobile workforce?
25. What are we doing to protect privacy and personally identifiable information, and how are we as a board ensuring that the right policies are in place? When and how are we using encryption?

Apple CEO Tim Cook recently said to the *Wall Street Journal*, "I don't know a way to protect people without encrypting. You can't have a back door that's only for the good guys."

According to a PricewaterhouseCoopers report titled *The Global State of Information Security*, businesses boosted their information security budgets by 24 percent in 2015, and most are investing in threat assessments, security standards, employee training and awareness, and a chief information-security officer to lead the way. In the boardroom, you can put measures in place, but there are also things you can do to prevent provocation or being a target yourself. Build your security dashboard and keep it up to date as a critical tool for oversight.

## SENIOR MANAGEMENT AND BOARD SOCIAL MEDIA—AND MOBILE DO'S AND DON'TS

As already mentioned, a key exposure area is social media, so it's worth a few more paragraphs to detail the importance of setting clear policies for critical personnel, executives, and board members. It's very easy to find out almost everything about a person by tracking his or her social-media activity. That's when a person becomes vulnerable for an attack. A fake e-mail or phone call with someone claiming to be from your company or an important vendor, your doctor's office, or customers needing personal information can lure you into trusting an attacker. When validated with some information about you that sounds plausible, he or she has just created an opening to dupe you.

Jennifer Wolfe

By checking LinkedIn, I can know everywhere you have worked, where you went to school, and even presentations you have given or what people say about you. From Facebook, I can see your family, your spouse, your kids, your relationship status, your vacations—everything about who you are as a person. If you tweet, I know what you are doing and thinking all day long. On Foursquare, I can see where you are and can geolocate you. And those are just the big ones, let alone the many emerging social-media sites that, combined, can tell me everything about you.

Edward Snowden is in exile because he thought that the US government snooping on American citizens was wrong. But millions of Americans *willingly* give away their sacred privacy each and every day for anyone to see on social media. When your senior management or board members are on social media, they are broadcasting all of the information the bad guys need to attack your company or trick you. Don't be fooled into thinking that anything you do online is private.

Generally, senior management and board members should limit the use of social media. If you are going to use it, you should have an account that does not clearly identify you by association with the company. If it does, you should very carefully manage it, and you should only engage with your closest and trusted friends. This means more than just not listing your job or affiliation, but possibly even using an alternate name or nickname. If I can look you up on social media and know where you work, then we have a problem: it is a potential for exposure.

If you have a LinkedIn profile, keep it private and only link with people you actually know. LinkedIn has convinced thousands of professionals to post their online résumés and keep them updated. But LinkedIn makes money by helping salespeople, among others, figure out how to mine all that data. For recruiters, it's a haven, but it's also one for bad guys who want to learn everything they need to know about your board and senior managers before attacking your company.

Only share with people you know or trust. Even then, be careful.

Also be careful on Facebook. The original social network has beefed up privacy settings in recent years, mindful of the concerns and potential for abuse. But be careful, because even if you aren't friends with someone, others can tag you in photos or mention you in their statuses, which can suck you into their feeds, and those, in turn, could be exposed to thousands of people. Even if you don't want to be tagged, and despite all the privacy settings, it's quite easy to search through Facebook and find components of someone's Facebook life by friending an unsuspecting friend of that person. Early adopters of Facebook likely friended a lot of people. If you want to continue to use Facebook, you might consider setting up a new account, keeping your circle very close, and setting higher privacy settings.

In all of these social media, remember that as a senior manager or board member, you are held to a higher standard than a typical employee. Everything you do and say represents your company and can expose you and your company to attacks. Keep in mind these basic social-media Dos and Don'ts:

# DO

* Limit information about your company, position, and activities on social media.
* Link in, like, follow, or connect only with people you actually know and trust. Carefully monitor and purge your connections.
* Limit social-media activities to a specific businesss purpose or carefully maintain separate personal social media accounts shared with only your most trusted friends and operated with discretion.
* If you use social media for strategic purposes, send only messages aligned with a corporate-messaging strategy.
* Regularly check your privacy settings to limit how people can see and access information about you. The default is no privacy. Have someone help you turn on every privacy setting possible in all social media you use. This includes on your phone and other devices.
* Consider how much social media you really need. Are there other ways to stay connected to the people you really care about in your life? Even if friends or family are far away, there are one-on-one ways of communicating that might save you some heartache and allow you more privacy in the most important personal relationships.

## DON'T

* Constantly post about where you are, when you are traveling, or who you are with.
* Make political statements unless this is something your company is strategically doing and you are aligned with that message.
* Use social media when you should be working. This creates a trail that can later come back to haunt you on many levels.
* Share information that could be clues to your passwords or give people a reason to blackmail you.

Unfortunately, using social media means that your personal life is difficult to separate from your work life. When you reach a position of power in an organization and serve in senior management or on the board, the price you pay is that you may not be able to live freely in a social-media-frenzied digital world. The risks of using social media can often outweigh the benefit.

## WILL STATUS-QUO CULTURE PREVENT YOU FROM KNOWING WHAT YOU NEED TO KNOW?

In chapters 1 and 2, I warned about status-quo thinking and how it sometimes prevents senior management from learning of new opportunities. The same is true for threats and particularly cyberattacks. According to the *International Business Times*, 60 percent of IT departments don't report small breaches unless the results are serious. This means that while new potential solutions or best practices may be introduced to your IT professionals and legal professionals or even discussed in digital operations, there is a good chance that, unless you create a culture to push for better cybersecurity programs and regularly independently audit those programs, you won't even be aware if there is an exposure.

What future technology could help with this issue? Are you developing it? Is someone else? What should you be thinking about in the future

## Digital in the Boardroom

to protect your business? Consider for a moment what I discussed in chapter 2—the big bang no one heard. I shared with you how these new Dot Brands or exclusive-access, top-level domains for companies could be one piece of the security puzzle. It's certainly only one piece, but is your cybersecurity plan looking at all ways to lock your doors? There are products and services that allow companies to protect, scan, and layer in protection to build out safe Internet spaces. If you build your internal systems in your Dot Brand space rather than a dot-com cloud environment, you can add layers of protection and insulate it further from public access. Is your IT team considering this, or just dismissing it? What other technologies or tools can you put in place?

I found that when I raised this issue with even some of the best network engineers in the world, they often initially dismissed it, but as I pushed with more questions, they reconsidered, saying it could work, but that they would need to think about it. Are your teams thinking about it? If you put someone in charge of cybersecurity who views the new technology or ideas as a potential threat to his or her job or turf, you will likely face resistance. This is why independent review and oversight is needed. Spend time in your board meetings discussing these issues. During your board retreat, dedicate time for in-depth conversation about them. Use outside help and expertise to integrate a holistic approach to digital, including cybersecurity. Consider more about how a status-quo mentality could be preventing you from learning about important trends or solutions that impact your company's future.

I provide a detailed, digital-best-practices list for boards in chapter 9, but the key question on cybersecurity is, do you have checks and balances? Do you audit your digital and cybersecurity operations? Audit has become such a critical function in aftermath of the Enron scandal. If the team auditing your cybersecurity is also head of your own IT department, you might not have real checks and balances. Below, I've compiled top security breaches of the last ten years, ranked by the target's market capitalization.

| Market Cap Rank | Company | Date | Nature of Breach |
|---|---|---|---|
| 1 | Apple Inc. | Feb. 2013; Sept. 2012 | In 2013, Apple detected malware, inserted by exploiting a flaw in Java, on computers of employees who visited a software developer site. (Similar breaches occurred at Facebook and Microsoft.) In 2012, "hacktivist" group Anonymous stole several unique iOS-powered device codes (which could be used to identify users), allegedly from the FBI, and uploaded them to the web. Apple made a public statement denying that it had provided data to the FBI. Eventually a small company in Florida admitted to a data breach that led to the leaked codes. |
| 2 | Exxon Mobil Corp. | June 2012; Feb. 2011 | Anonymous targeted ExxonMobil and other oil companies (Shell, BP, Gazprom, and Rosneft) in an environmental campaign, claiming to have leaked more than three hundred ExxonMobil employee e-mail addresses and passwords, but the company would not confirm the breach. In 2011, hackers stole proprietary information from Exxon-Mobil's network, resulting in a loss of financing information related to oil- and gas-field bids and operations. |
| 3 | Google Inc. | June 2011; 2009 | In 2011, Google announced that Gmail accounts of some members of the US government had been compromised by Chinese hackers. In 2009, Chinese hackers exploited a weakness in an old version of Internet Explorer to access Google's internal network and steal some intellectual property. |
| 4 | Microsoft Corp. | Feb. 2013 | Microsoft announced that a number of employee devices were infected by malware installed by exploiting a flaw in Java while employees downloaded material from unsafe websites. Microsoft found no evidence of customer data being affected. |
| 5 | Wal-mart Stores Inc. | 2005 & 2006 | Hackers accessed Walmart's point-of-sale computer system and stole source code. Walmart informed federal law enforcement but did not publicly disclose the breach because it saw no evidence of tampering with consumer information. |
| 6 | General Electric | 2010 | Private cybersecurity firm HBGary Federal was hacked, and thousands of HBGary e-mails were released to the public. These e-mails revealed that General Electric was the target of cyber-security attacks. |
| 7 | Johnson & Johnson | 2010 | In the same HBGary Federal hacking, e-mails revealed that Johnson & Johnson was the target of cybersecurity attacks. |
| 8 | Chevron Corporation | 2010 | Stuxnet, the sophisticated computer virus created by the United States and Israel to use against Iran, infected Chevron's network, but Chevron said that it suffered no adverse effects. |
| 9 | Intl. Business Machines | Jan. 2011 | An IBM site for developers was defaced by hackers who replaced web pages with their own messages warning that the website was still vulnerable. . |
| 10 | Wells Fargo & Company | Late 2012; Aug. 2008 | In 2012, Wells Fargo was one of many US banks (also including BofA, Citigroup, U.S. Bancorp, PNC, and Capital One) to experience major disruptions to their online banking sites as a result of distributed denial-of-service attacks. No bank accounts were breached, and no customer money was accessed. In 2008, Wells Fargo told customers that hackers had accessed confidential personal data (including names, addresses, dates of birth, social security numbers, driver's license numbers, and some credit card information) by illegally obtaining the company's access codes. |
| 11 | Procter & Gamble Co. | May 2011 | Hacker 4Chan made counterfeit coupons for various products. $200,000 worth of Tide coupons were redeemed at stores even though P&G had never created a download-and-print coupon. |
| 12 | Pfizer, Inc. | July 2011 | Pfizer had to take down its official Facebook page after it was hacked by activists who posted unauthorized content. Pfizer did not say how the page was accessed, but it may have been through an employee of a third-party vendor that claimed Pfizer as a social media client. |
| 13 | JPMorgan Chase & Co. | Mar. 2013 | JPMorgan Chase's website was taken offline for about a day through a hacker's denial-of-service attack. |

## Digital in the Boardroom

| Market Cap Rank | Company | Date | Nature of Breach |
|---|---|---|---|
| 16 | HSBC Holdings | Oct. 2012 | HSBC websites were taken down by a denial-of-service attack, leaving some sites inaccessible for several hours. HSBC released a statement that the attacks affected customers worldwide, but that sensitive account data was not exposed. |
| 17 | AT&T Inc. | Apr. 2010 | A hacker revealed a security hole on AT&T's website by obtaining personal information for 120,000 iPad users who had signed up for AT&T data service. The hacker obtained e-mail addresses for high-profile early iPad users such as Michael Bloomberg and Rahm Emanuel, as well as many Department of Defense and Homeland Security employees. |
| 18 | Toyota Motor Corp. Ltd. | Aug. 2012 | Toyota filed a federal lawsuit against former IT contractor of its United States based manufacturing company, alleging that the contractor logged onto Toyota's system after he was fired and downloaded and printed trade secrets related to ToyotaSupplier.com, a website where its suppliers exchange highly sensitive information with the company about current and future products. Toyota clamed that if the information stolen was made public, it would suffer "immediate and irreparable damage." |
| 20 | Coca-Cola Company | Mar. 2009 | Hackers sent e-mail to company executives containing malware and were able to break into Coca-Cola's computer system and steal sensitive files related to it's attempted $2.4-billion acquisition of a Chinese juice company. Hackers made daily intrusions into the network over a period of at least one month. The deal collapsed a few days after the FBI informed Coca-Cola of the breach. |
| 49 | Comcast Corp. NBC | Feb. 2013; Mar. 2012 | in 2013, NBC.com was attacked by malware (Citadel Trojan) most likely to steal usernames, passwords, and other personal info. In 2012, a hacker posted e-mail addresses, passwords, and ID numbers online. |
| 109 | Facebook, Inc. | Feb. 2013 | Facebook found malware on a number of employee laptops after a few employees visited a mobile developer website that turned out to be unsafe. Hackers had exploited a vulnerability in Java and accessed some data, but Facebook found no evidence that user data was compromised. |
| 167 | TJX Companies | Dec. 2006 | Ninety-four million credit cards were exposed through a breach of TJX's network, which was not protected by any firewalls. |
| 168 | Capital One Financial Corporation | Nov. 2011 | Anonymous claimed an attack on Capital One Bank's website and published personal information about high-profile corporate executives and billionaires, such as Michael Bloomberg and Carlos Slim. Capital One said its website disruptions resulted from routine maintenance. |
| 218 | Yahoo! Inc. | July 2012 | Hackers were able to attack Yahoo!'s networks by exploiting a flaw and downloading 450,000 plain-text log-in credentials. Yahoo! was subsequently sued for negligence after the attack. The hackers posted: "We hope the parties responsible for managing the security of this subdomain will take this as a wake-up call, and not as a threat." |
| 228 | CBS Corporation | Apr. 2013; Jan. 2012 | In 2013, multiple CBS News Twitter accounts were hacked and used to distribute false headlines about the U.S. providing weapons of mass destruction to Syria. Many users who clicked on the links to false news stories had their computers infected with malware.<br>In 2012, CBS.com was hacked by Anonymous after the U.S. government cracked down on file-sharing site megaupload.com |
| 686 | Burger King World Wide Inc. | Feb. 2013 | Burger King's Twitter feed was hacked to report (for over an hour) the fake sale of Burger King to its biggest competitor, McDonalds. Although BK picked up many new twitter followers after the hack, it made the company look bad for its lack of control over Twitter. |

Figures 3.4A and 3.4B (Top cybersecurity breaches)

## KEY TAKEAWAYS FROM CHAPTER 3

* A cyberattack has likely already occurred or will occur in your organization.
* Boards are being held to a higher standard, and the Securities and Exchange Commission may soon mandate oversight of cybersecurity.
* Understand why you might be attacked and how, and put in place mitigation plans.
* Recognize that you, your employees, and your vendors are the weakest links. A breach is not usually a sophisticated hack but often a door or window left open by someone who innocently lets in the bad guys by downloading a file or clicking an e-mailed link.
* Audit, prepare, practice—and repeat. Cybersecurity is ongoing, though the tools and tactics will change. Have a plan, create a dashboard, and be proactive in preparation, because it's not a matter of if, but when.
* Train board members, senior managers, and key employees about potential threats and how to use social media, mobile, and online more safely.

*Chapter 4*

## SEARCH REWIRED

As we continue around the digital map of your organization, we inevitably arrive at search-engine optimization. This is probably something you don't spend a lot of time thinking about, leaving it to the experts. But understanding how navigation of the Internet works and how search is continually evolving will be important for identifying future trends in the digital space, particularly with regard to reengineering your digital neighborhood for better security and results.

This chapter provides a brief history of how search formed and has worked. I want to help you understand what's changing and what's most important.

You may remember the early days of the Internet, when you accessed websites exclusively through browsers on your desktop computer. Back then, companies created their home pages to serve as home bases for the Internet experience. There wasn't much to the early web presence. Take a look at this early-stage website—it was essentially just an index of links to other information.

In the beginning, to find anything on the Internet, you had to be a techie. You had to understand Archie, Veronica, and other early search engines. Google emerged as the search giant by creating a simple home page with a powerful algorithm behind it that was designed to make sense of this massive Internet space for anyone, not just the techies.

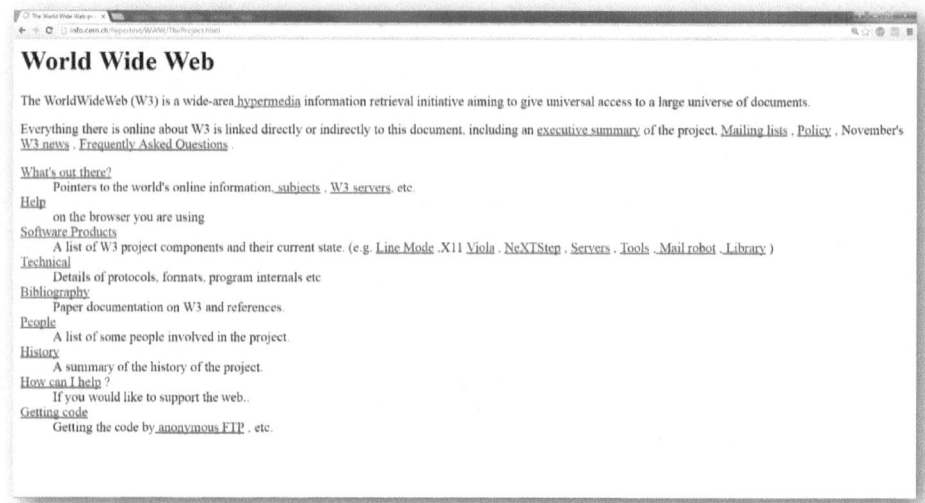

Fig. 4.1. Early website

If you go to Google's archives (http://searchengineland.com/the-top-7-milestones-of-google-search-173578. Also see www.Boardroom.Solutions) you'll see that the original search page hasn't changed much. It's gotten cleaner and simpler, but the concept remains the same: type in what you are looking for, and Google produces the results. That's what we experience as consumers on the front ends of our computers and devices.

Google is one of the few companies that hasn't needed to change its home page much over the years, because the page has been singularly focused on a simple premise—offer consumers the best search engine on the planet to help them find what they want in a vastly expanding Internet universe. The page didn't have to change much, because as Google created new product offerings, it built out microsites and other pages for them rather than clutter up the home page—a lesson most businesses could take: keep the home page simple and clean. Other businesses have built massive home pages as hubs for spokes—thousands or even millions of subpages and spaces in the Internet universe. Sound confusing if you wanted to find something? It was—and is. So what was the answer? A Google search to cut through the clutter was the best way to search amid thousands of possible landing pages.

As the average consumer came to rely upon Google as the guide to the Internet, companies quickly realized that they needed to rank highly in

### Digital in the Boardroom

Google's organic search so that people would find their businesses—instead of others'—online. We immediately witnessed a new industry form around the need for companies to uncover how to rank higher in search engines; it's referred to as search-engine optimization (SEO). Marketers quickly learned that average consumers would not look past the first page of search results, so getting to the top of the list became critically important.

Of course, today, search occurs across platforms—from desktop computers, mobile devices, and tablets all the way to Internet TV, where the platforms we use (such as Apple TV, Roku, or Amazon Fire) can control the messaging and prompts we now receive and how we search within their catalogs of content choices. And today, we battle for app position on devices.

Search has been rewired over and over again throughout the last fifteen years to respond to not just Google's changing algorithm, but also how consumers actually use and navigate this ever-expanding Internet universe. In fact, Google frequently says in its blogs that the company evolves search to be the best there is to help people find what they want. In studying Google's algorithm changes, one can see historically that the company actually responds to what's happening out there in the Internet universe. According to Matt Cutts, Google's longtime blogger and voice of search,

If you keep the mental model of "What is Google trying to do?"—trying to return great search results for users—then that helps you try to align yourself with those goals. If you are aligned with those goals, then we are trying to return the high quality pages that you are making. If you aren't aligned with those goals, you are always going to be working in opposition to the algorithms, and you're always going to be working in opposition to regular users and what they want to see. (https://www.youtube.com/watch?v=8AFTR5rsUAI. Also see www.boardroom.solutions)

In the boardroom, you may not be all that concerned about how your company's website is optimized or how its digital world is created. You are likely much more concerned with the financial numbers of the organization and holding the leadership accountable to the stockholders, as you should. But in the changing digital environment, how your company manages this vast Internet space is increasingly important to how you respond to disruptive changes and prepare for the future as well as how you protect yourself from attacks. If you are in the boardroom and don't understand the basics of how this all works, then you could miss important signals to the future of the business. I'll break this down into a few simple formulas.

## SEO MADE SIMPLE

How effectively consumers find the information you want them to find about you depends on what happens in two big categories: the "front of the house" and the "back of the house."

**Front of the house.** This is what consumers see, read, and experience when they visit your digital world: quality content, good graphics, changing content. What a searcher is looking for is really what that space should be all about. In general, the front of the house needs to be a good, clean space that delivers quality content. This means that the content is original to you, always fresh, and changing; it is accurate, grammatical, and written well. The visitor sees a nice, clean page that is easy to read, with good graphics and video. In other words, the front of the house is about delivering Internet users good content in an easy-to-digest manner. Front of the house also takes into account social-media relevance and general web popularity (i.e., the more traffic you have, the more likely you are to be found—it is a chicken-and-egg situation).

**Back of the house.** This is how your site is organized and developed. What happens here is a bit more technical, so I'll be brief. Back of the house is really what your web developers and engineers do to boost the optimization value and index value of your digital properties. It's much more about how the code is written, how links are structured, and how elegantly your digital pages are constructed.

What's important to keep in mind here is that everything is integrated. So, what you do in social media and mobile impacts the front and back of the house from a user-experience and index perspective. In the latest SEO books and articles, a few checklists emerge for constructing the back and the front of the house; the graphic shows one example.

I'm sure that these details may not have a lot of meaning for you, and that's OK, but what is important to recognize is that everything is connected in the digital world, and what you do in one place directly impacts another. We've seen so many changes that simply adding the latest SEO strategy onto an already overburdened home page doesn't make a lot of sense. What may be most helpful in giving you an edge when the techies start going on and on about SEO topics is to have a fundamental understanding of how search on the Internet works. Many of the same principles apply today that applied years ago, except the environment is just bigger and more complex.

In the early days, there were not as many websites as there are today, so searching was a little easier. There was less for an algorithm to crawl through. Google was just getting started. No one knew exactly how a company that provided a search engine for free was going to make money. When Google started its ad program in October of 2000, the need for organic search versus ad-based placement was born. While some viewed it as a way to "game the system," others quickly came to learn that it was a matter of survival for their businesses. Online businesses emerged faster than we could keep up, and they all depended upon traffic to their sites to reach the critical masses they needed.

In December 1995, 16 million people on Planet Earth used the Internet. By 2014, there were 3,079 million people using the Internet, which still only represented 42.4 percent of the world's population. In 1995, there were about 23,500 domain names or websites. Today, there are more than 700 million websites. To find something on the Internet, we go to Google, Bing, or Yahoo!, or one of many other search engines to start a query.

Search engines, then and now, have four functions:

1. Crawling websites
2. Building indexes
3. Calculating relevancy and ranking
4. Serving results

Many factors influence where a site appears in web-search results.

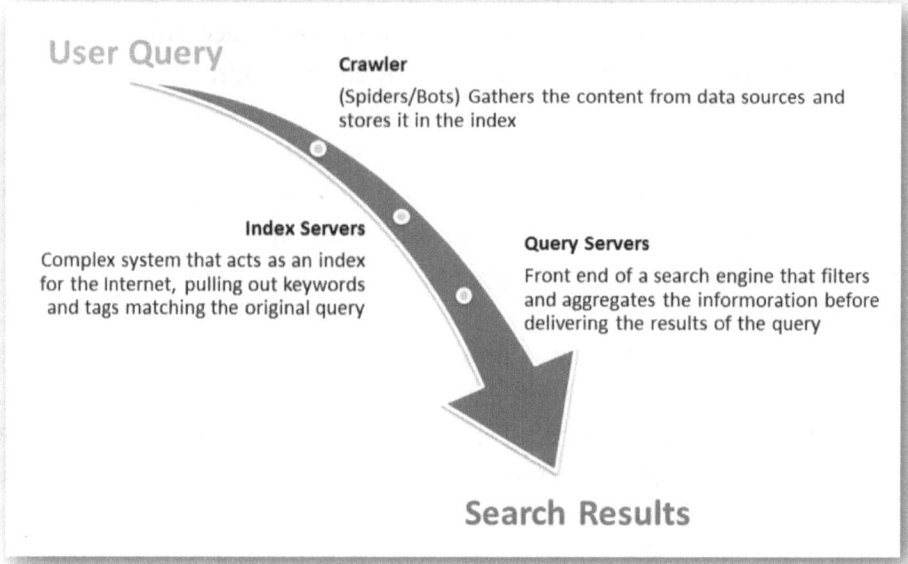

Fig. 4.2. How search works

Early search engines each held an index of a few hundred thousand pages and documents and received one or two thousand inquiries each day. Today, a top search engine indexes hundreds of millions of pages and respond to tens of millions of queries per day.

**Web crawling.** Before a search engine can tell you where a file or document is, it must find it. To find information on the hundreds of millions of web pages (and now other digital properties) that exist, a search engine employs special software robots, called spiders, to build lists of the words found on websites. The process of a spider building its lists is called web crawling. To build and maintain a useful list of words, a search engine's spiders have to look at a lot of pages. The usual starting points for spiders are lists of heavily used servers and very popular pages.

A spider begins with a popular site, indexing the words on its pages and following every link found within the site. The spider system then quickly travels, spreading out across the most widely used portions of the web. Note that popularity has always been a key indicator to a spider that something should be ranked higher. Telling companies how to become popular is what keeps a lot of digital agencies in business.

Google began as an academic search engine. In the paper that describes how the system was built, Sergey Brin and Larry Page give an example of how quickly their spiders worked. They built their initial system to use multiple spiders, usually three at once. Each spider could keep about three hundred connections to web pages open at a time. At its peak performance, using four spiders, their system could crawl over a hundred pages per second, generating around six hundred kilobytes of data each second. Keeping everything running quickly meant building a system to feed necessary information to the spiders.

The early Google system had a server dedicated to providing URLs to the spiders. Rather than depending on an Internet-service provider for the domain-name server (DNS) that translates a server's name into an address, Google had its own DNS to keep delays to a minimum. When the Google spider looked at a page, it took note of two things: the words within the page and where the words were found.

Words occurring in the title, subtitles, meta tags, and other positions of relative importance were noted for special consideration during a subsequent user search. The Google spider was built to index every significant word on a page, leaving out the articles *a*, *an*, and *the*.

Other spiders take different approaches. These different approaches usually attempt to make the spider operate faster and allow users to search more efficiently, or both. For example, some spiders keep track of the words in the title, subheadings, and links along with the hundred most frequently used words on the page and each word in the first twenty lines of text.

Based on spider approaches, early SEO tactics included the following:

* In the visible page text, use words that users might choose as search-query terms to find the information on your site.

    Give the site a clear hierarchy and text links.

- * Make sure that each page is accessible by at least one static text link.
- * Limit all pages to a reasonable size. One topic per page.
- * Don't put the text that you want indexed in side images.
- * Make pages primarily for users, not for search engines. Don't deceive your users or present different content to search engines than you display to users (a practice referred to as cloaking).

  Create a useful, information-rich site and write pages that clearly and accurately describe your content.
- * Keep the links on a given page to a reasonable number—fewer than a hundred.

These basic fundamentals can help set the stage for making predictions about future optimization. You can imagine over the years how these criteria have changed and that armies of people in your companies and agencies have been tacking on changes to your home page and subpages year after year after year to get better and better at being found.

Meta tags allow the owner of a page to specify keywords and concepts under which the page will be indexed. This can be helpful when the words on the page might have double or triple meanings—the meta tags can guide the search engine in choosing which of the several possible meanings for these words is correct. However, a careless or unscrupulous page owner might add meta tags that fit very popular topics but have nothing to do with the actual contents of the page, so to protect against this, spiders correlate meta tags with page content, rejecting meta tags that don't match the words on the page.

**Building the index.** Once the spiders have completed the task of finding information on web pages, the search engine must store the information in a way that makes it useful. There are two key components involved in making the gathered data accessible to users: the information stored with the data and the method by which the information is indexed.

Each search engine has a different formula for assigning weight to the words in its index. This is one of the reasons that a search for the same word on different search engines produces different lists and pages presented in different orders. An index has a single purpose: it allows information to be found as quickly as possible. You'll find, for example, that the *A* section of the dictionary is much thicker than the *X* section. This inequity means that finding a word beginning with a very popular letter could take much longer than finding a word that begins with a less popular one. The combination of efficient indexing and effective storage makes it possible to get results quickly, even when the user creates a complicated search.

It's within this concept that the integration of social media, mobile platforms, and the new generic top-level domains start to have an impact. If you are searching just within Facebook, you are searching a smaller universe than the entire Internet. Or, you may be searching only within your friend network. If you are searching for apps, you are searching in an app store, an even smaller universe. And, in the new top-level domain space, if you search within more segmented spaces, the number of sites to crawl may be smaller and you may more easily find what you are looking for.

**Calculating relevancy and ranking.** This is the part where the search algorithm comes in. Once the digital property has been crawled and indexed, the algorithm is ready to perform its magic—to calculate if it's relevant to what the searcher is seeking and then rank the results. I've included a bit more on the algorithms below, but this is the *secret sauce* of what differentiates one search engine from another and isn't always made publicly available. Most of the search engines put out briefings about how to rank high in their searches, and that's a lot of what I've included here, but they change those criteria regularly.

**Serving results.** Finally, here's the part where consumers come in. We get the results page. Bing changed the approach to delivering results to make it much more graphic. Of course, Google also now has multiple ways to review results—either graphically, or in traditional word form, or even on maps. This is where we will see great innovation in the future as our devices evolve around our lives and become flat panels on our walls or furniture or embedded into our homes, cars, and everything we do. How search results are delivered will be an interesting game to watch in the future.

## THE TRADITIONAL APPROACH TO SEO—HOW TO GET THE ALGORITHM TO FIND YOU AND RANK YOU

Companies take specific steps to utilize their SEO strategies to the fullest in an expanding Internet environment. Traditionally, it was all about pay per click. To be number one, you had to pay for it. This created an oligarchy in which big companies could dominate search engines—so people who were producing great content but lacked the monetary resources could only be found below the paying advertisers. In the early days, one-page optimization was the focus—what you did within your website to come up higher in the rankings. Today, as I'll cover in the coming chapters, it's just as much about what you do on your page as what you do out in the social-media and mobile spaces.

To rank high these days, there are a few crucial criteria. Some of the top criteria on Google's search included the following:

1. Number of other sites linking to your site
2. Quality of the site
3. Content of the pages
4. Updates made to indices
5. A keyword in the domain as a relevancy signal
6. Domain age
7. Domain-name length
8. Public versus private whois (what information is provided about who owns the website to ICANN and whether it is publicly available)
9. Country codes (which tend to limit a site's ability to rank globally)
10. Page-loading speed via HTML
11. Whether its content duplicates content elsewhere (which can negatively affect search results)
12. Image optimization
13. Recency of content updates
14. Outbound link quality and theme
15. Quality of grammar and spelling
16. No copied content

17. Internal links pointing to pages
18. Quality of internal links
19. Reading level (intermediate preferred)
20. Appropriate amount of information on the contact page
21. Site architecture (silo structures help organize content)

Additionally, the other major search engines, such as Bing, Yahoo!, or, in China, Baidu, follow similar guidelines. They each put out regular statements about how to rank well in their search engines.

## METADATA

Another early tool of SEO gurus was the use of metadata, or words buried in the HTML (hypertext markup language—the code behind the website) tags themselves. When layering keywords or competitor names into the metadata or the coding of the website, site builders hoped that the algorithms might spot them and think they were part of the site. This was a big way to game the system and spurred numerous lawsuits by trademark owners wanting to stop competitors from layering their sites with meta tags containing trademarked names.

In the middle of the last decade, this practice resulted in web searches for specific trademarks returning not only the trademark holder's site, but also competitors' sites that had buried the trademarked name in their metadata. Before a law on this was codified, everyone moved away from the technique: search engines moved away from relying on it because it was too easy to abuse and thus not all that useful to site owners anymore. Once search engines stopped caring, people stopped doing it, and the litigation stopped. This means that we never really got a clear answer on whether the use of the trademark in unseen metadata infringed the rights in that trademark.

The early strategy on metadata was that each page had to have its own tags, or the search engines would penalize the page owner. In the past, SEO experts would mine through pages and pages of a website to determine if it was properly tagged to meet the current algorithm, but that has changed. According to Matt Cutts, "Google uses over two hundred signals in our web search rankings, but the keyword's meta tag is not currently one of them, and I don't believe it will be."

This all gave rise to the concept of white-hat versus black-hat SEO tactics.

## WHITE-HAT SEO VERSUS BLACK-HAT SEO

White-hat SEO included approved strategies for getting a page to rank well. Google would actually publish what these strategies were and post blogs in which they answered questions about them. Google actually posts Webmaster guidelines (https://support.google.com/webmasters/answer/35769?hl=en&ref_topic=6002025. Also see www.boardroom.solutions). Black-hat strategies include those that Google does not like and would penalize. This includes keyword stuffing and backlinking (using software to generate tens of thousands of backlinks to your site).

Fig. 4.3. White-hat and black-hat SEO tactics

## Digital in the Boardroom

In the last fifteen years, we have gone from an age of search words, backlinks, and metadata to a focus on high-quality content and delivering to customers what they want in a more tailored and niched way, not just on web properties, but across the digital ecosphere.

But now, so many changes have transformed the digital world that we can't just keep redesigning the home page or applying new SEO tactics or creating mobile sites or building out microsites somewhere within the architecture of our domain spaces or creating more and more Facebook pages and Twitter accounts. The very purpose of the online experience has changed from when it began. It's time to rethink it all and build out a digital world that delivers something that matters. Before we do, let's look at the continued evolution of the search algorithm for historical perspective. Take a look at the major Google algorithm changes over the last twelve years:

# Google
## Algorithm Changes Since 2003

- **2003** — Backlinks. Crackdown on black hat tactics
- **2004** — Crackdown on Metatag stuffing
- **2005** — End of link farms; evolution into user's search history
- **2006** — Updates to supplemental index and filtered pages
- **2007** — Integration with news, video, images, local
- **2008** — Unspecified changes to search index
- **2009** — Twitter, google news and new content integrated to real time feed
- **2010** — Crackdown on low quality pages, new web indexing system
- **2011** — Crackdown on thin content and content farms; emphasis on recent content - Panda - Big Impact
- **2012** — More localization, crackdown on link and keyword schemes - Penguin - Big Impact
- **2013** — High Quality content and full question searches: Hummingbird - Big Impact
- **2014** — Pigeon - Focus on local and stronger ties to search signals and contextual intelligence
- **2015** — Mobilegeddon - Websites with responsive designs are now favored in search rankings.

Fig. 4.4. Google algorithm history

## THE FUTURE

The one key theme we can always see in looking at Google's algorithm history is that it's doing two things:

1. Always trying to improve to give people what they want. Google truly wants to deliver the best possible core product to consumers. That's why the home page hasn't changed in fifteen years.
2. Responding to what's happening in the Internet universe. As we have become more sophisticated about what we want on websites in terms of content, Google has responded. When we didn't want to end up on bad sites with old, repurposed, or stolen content, Google responded. When we started using social media, Google responded. When we started using mobile, Google responded. Every year, Google responds to what's going on out there.

Matt Cutts stated:

If you keep the mental model of "What is Google trying to do?"— trying to return great search results for users—then that helps you try to align yourself with those goals. If you are aligned with those goals, then we are trying to return the high quality pages that you are making. If you aren't aligned with those goals, you are always going to be working in opposition to the algorithms and you're always going to be working in opposition to regular users and what they want to see. (https://www.youtube.com/watch?v=8AFTR5rsUAI. Also see www.boardroom.solutions.)

Today, Google's algorithm is a semantic-search-based system delivering answers, not just links. Google's algorithm *actually* thinks now, and it does so with contextual intelligence. This is why integration with social and mobile is so important. The algorithms have gotten smarter—more like people—so we can no longer rely on old tactics. SEO expert and author, David Amerland, explains, "'Semantic' is a Greek word that means 'meaning,' and the field of

Semantics busies itself with the study of the meaning of the words and the anthology of logic.

> "In search on the web, semantic search marks the transition from a "dumb" search of single web pages that have a probabilistic value of containing the information we are looking for to an intelligent search that delivers real answers or leads us to the very answer we are looking for on a web page that has nothing to do with the search query we used and therefore would not have come up in the traditional keyword-activated results of the past."

Google's algorithm is pulling all of the pieces together. It knows who you are, your GPS geolocation, the GPS signal on your phone, the address of what you are looking for, and reviews about it. It knows what social networks you frequent and what you do. It knows which mobile device you are using. It knows all of this about you. So, when you search for a restaurant or a place to order flowers or to do anything, it's pulling all of this information in addition to what you type, not just the words.

Google's Cutts stated: "Start to think about mobile. If you look at your analytics, you will see an exponential curve that shows mobile users will surpass desktop users in the next 2–3 years. You want to make it so that the user's interests and the search engine's interests are as aligned as possible." (https://www.youtube.com/watch?v=vnFCGqySlv8. Also see www.boardroom.solutions)

Google is using its new methods to compartmentalize search—new top-level domains will help further by creating authentic spaces for the search engines to recognize. This is one more reason that your company will want to have a new Dot Brand. When Google's semantic search engine recognizes that your company's Dot Brand is the one true you and that the searcher is looking for you, everything your company builds in that space will be authenticated. This is why gaming the system with words, links, and so on just won't work anymore. It's all connected, and the algorithms are getting smarter and smarter. So, using a technology platform like a Dot Brand instead of just a domain name makes sense. It's why Google itself has pursued so many new top-level domains.

It's also why some of these new spaces that provide more natural language will fit nicely into the future of search—it all ties together into niched areas. These natural-language domains could prove to be more valuable. For example, finddirect.flights, crowdfunding.works, devour.life, cold.solutions, freshfromthe.farm, healthyliving.solutions, modern.works, smartdream.house, southern.life, startup.life, and stain.solutions—they're all more natural-language-based domain names. If I apply the other SEO tactics and build out good content tailored to a specific market for a specific purpose, it's likely that semantic-based search is going to pick up on that. As voice recognition and search evolves how you ask your device to find something for you, algorithms that predict behavior and natural-language-based digital addresses may transform how search is conducted altogether.

Amazon can predict what we might want to buy based upon our histories, locations, and even the weather forecast. This is also why understanding what the digital experience is in the digital world your company provides is so critical. You have to be able to define what you are providing. One home page is no longer going to cut it in search. Different landing pages for different content functions are essential—a digital address can help to answer a question, but only if your company designs it that way.

We've reached a point when it's time to rewire your entire digital neighborhood with a deeper understanding of how search works today and the path it's on for the future. It's important to really think and understand how you create the digital world so that the algorithms can help people find you—not lead them to a competitor. Always keep the searcher—your target audience—at the forefront of your thinking about strategy.

Build your authority, understand how your reputation is created and reinforced, and integrate all of your activities to make sure who you are as a company is transparent. As the algorithm becomes smarter, it will become savvier in *judging* whether you are authentic or not.

As a board member, you may find this all a bit too much in the weeds, and understandably so. But hopefully, this has given you a baseline understanding of how search has changed and will continue to change and how it may be time for a strategic digital overhaul at your organization. Too many companies are battling legacy architecture to the digital world. In the C-suite and boardroom, you can make the call for a fresh look or a redesign on a blank canvas, knowing what you know now. "What will be important, today and moving forward, is embracing the mix, getting the mix right, and repeating that success using these newer tactics. For a business to really achieve success, they have to look beyond the search engine and set their sights firmly on impressing the customer," says Duane Forrester, Webmaster for Bing at Microsoft. http://www.bing.com/blogs/site_blogs/b/webmaster/archive/2014/04/24/is-seo-the-future-no-and-here-s-why.aspx. Also see www.boardroom.solutions.)

As you continue on in your journey toward digital in the boardroom, consider that SEO can be complicated in a vast, new digital world. You can rely upon experts to give you advice and help you structure your digital world. But *you* need to provide the leadership to reengineer and reimagine the space. With a basic understanding of how the Internet landscape is changing, how search has evolved, and how cybersecurity threatens your organization, let's turn now to look at social and mobile.

## KEY TAKEAWAYS FROM CHAPTER 4

* How people search is about more than just the words they type in—it's now cross platform and cross device and spans across the digital world. Optimization is about more than just a single website. It's about optimizing your entire digital ecosphere.
* Leadership is needed to rethink and reengineer your digital world for the next generation of optimization. In the past, most organizations just kept plugging holes or solving problems—it's been nearly twenty years since most companies started using the Internet; it's time for a refreshed architecture of the space.
* Search engines will continue to change to use available data and information to get smarter and deliver people what they want. It may

evolve into more voice recognition and continue to use semantic-based search.
* Voice recognition tied to smarter algorithms could change the way search works in the future, but the underlying principles will remain the same.
* In the boardroom, having a cursory understanding of how search algorithms work will help you respond to how people may navigate the vast digital landscape in the future.

*Chapter 5*

## THE SOCIAL-NETWORK REVOLUTION: WHEN THE PEOPLE TOOK OVER

Facebook was introduced in February of 2004 by Mark Zuckerberg and a small battalion of Harvard students as an exclusive, online club for students to share photos and status updates. You've likely heard the story or seen the movie *The Social Network*. A decade later, Facebook has changed the world. As the digital platform for revolutions during the Arab Spring and the campaign strategy that won an election twice for President Obama, Facebook gave birth to the social-media generation. You may not be a Facebook or Twitter fanatic, but you surely understand their impact. When Ellen DeGeneres tweeted a selfie she took during the Oscars, the tweet was viewed by thirty-seven million people. Only forty-three million watched the awards show.

The virality of social media has transformed the way marketers think about their messaging and how they connect with their target consumers. It's no longer a one-way communication with ads blasted out to a specific demographic in a specific medium. It is now a one-to-many conversation that is controlled by the people and what they like or don't like. Social media has given a voice to the masses. The people have taken over. In the golden age of *Mad Men*, advertisers and companies created messages, and the masses simply absorbed them. But today, the people are creating the trends, driving the messages, and calling out companies and individuals whom they do not like, and corporations are scurrying to keep up with it all.

## Digital in the Boardroom

With the rise of social media came agencies and consultants telling executives they needed to get with the times and start using the new social platforms. But that advice may have been premature, for now we know that the price we pay for this connectivity is our privacy. And in the upper echelons of corporations and inside the boardrooms, where strategic decisions are made about the futures of companies, the need for privacy is greater than ever.

In the boardroom, it's important to understand the ways in which social media impacts how consumers navigate their digital worlds and what that means for your company's bottom line, but it's also important to understand how to leverage the massive amount of data being gathered about what everyone does online and what you should and shouldn't do in your individual capacity in social media. What's important? What's not? Are all of those Twitter accounts real? Can a Twitter war with Donald Trump or Kim Kardashian really take down a Fortune 500 company or executive? Who could possibly keep up with all of those tweets in the inbox every day? It takes a lot more than just using social media to understand how to harness its real power. In this chapter, I'll break it down into what you really need to know, as a director, about social media.

But to start, let's take a look at a few of the bigger Twitter wars. We all certainly expect celebrities to engage in the war of the wit on Twitter—their livelihoods and in-the-moment need for continued attention to maintain celebrity status depend upon it. But what about CEOs—surely they wouldn't reduce themselves to that? They would. Sprint CEO Marcelo Claure started a war of words on Twitter with rival T-Mobile chief John Legere.

Sprint continued the drama by citing a study placing them in third place in overall performance on CNBC. Legere lashed out on Twitter.

While some may argue that this exchange bought both companies a lot of free publicity, it is one indication of how a CEO or senior executive without counsel or board input could start a social-media tempest. And it's not just American telecom companies going at it. Donald Trump famously engages in Twitter wars with his competitors, from Mark Cuban and Rosie O'Donnell to political opponents. Trump uses war on Twitter to gain media attention and further his image, which is good for him, but may not be good for *your* company. What image is it creating? And is that what you want? These are really the key questions to answer before taking to social media for attention.

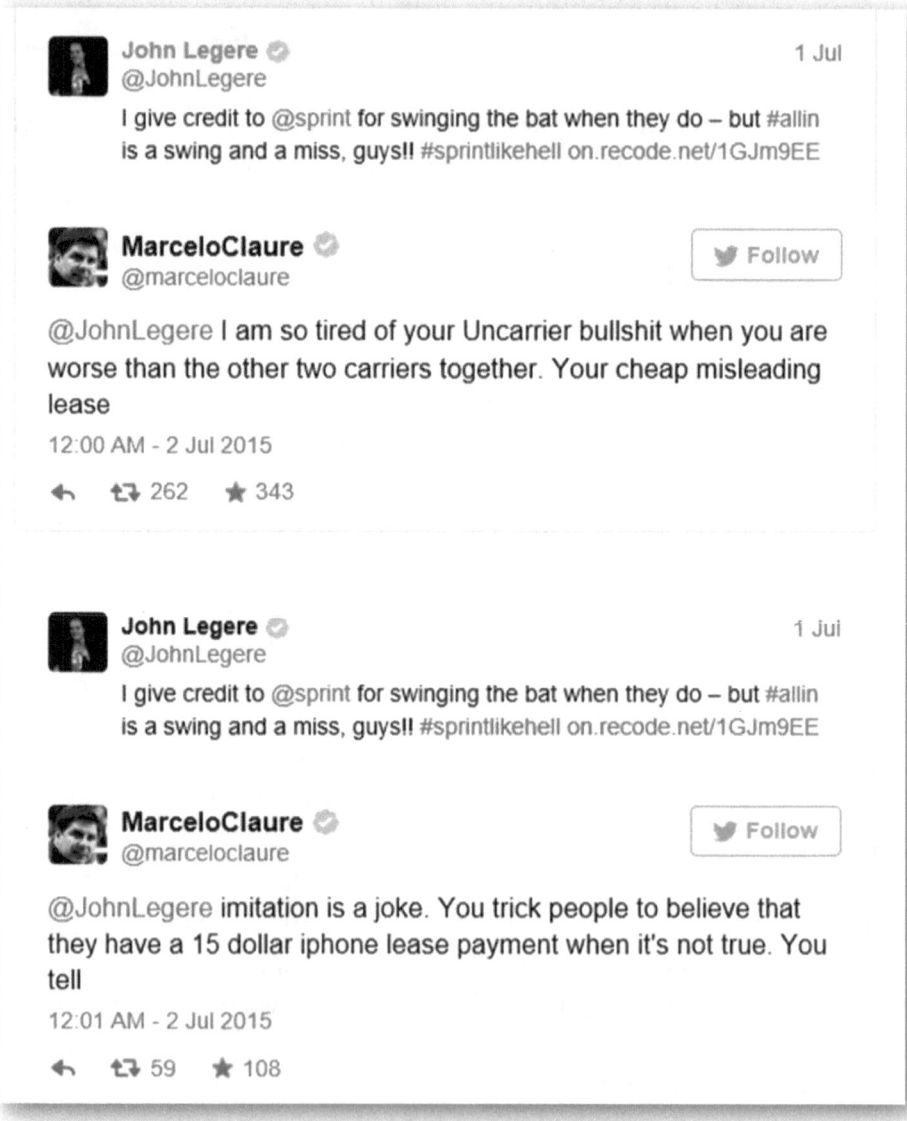

Fig. 5.2. Twitter wars, Part 2

Beyond bantering among CEOs, social media can produce damaging results. In 2014, ISIS threatened terrorist attacks on Twitter employees for shutting down accounts linked to the terrorist group. So even if Twitter attempts to regulate hate messages, it can quickly become a target. This situation exemplifies why caution is due in social media, particularly from senior executives who can speak on behalf of the company.

Also alarming is when companies' social-media managers potentially don't understand the implications of what they think are harmless tweets or posts. To celebrate the Fourth of July, American Apparel posted to its Tumblr page a stylized image of the space shuttle *Challenger*'s explosion. The company said it happened because its social media manager was born after the tragedy and thought the photo was of fireworks—a plausible explanation, but still a painful mistake. Companies may need more rigorous checks and balances and management of social media.

## WHICH SOCIAL PLATFORMS MATTER?

Let's start with the basics: which social platforms matter for companies. We surveyed the top Fortune 100 companies in 2015 to determine which social-media platforms they promote on their digital properties (see Figure 5.3). The most prevalent included Facebook, Twitter, LinkedIn, Pinterest, YouTube, and Instagram.

1. Walmart
2. Exxon Mobil
3. Chevron
4. Berkshire Hathaway
5. Apple - none
6. General Motors
7. Phillips 66
8. General Electric
9. Ford Motor
10. CVS Health
11. McKesson
12. AT&T
13. Valero Energy
14. UnitedHealth Group
15. Verizon
16. AmerisourceBergen
17. Fannie Mae
18. Costco - none
19. HP
20. Kroger
21. JP Morgan Chase
22. Express Scripts Holding
23. Bank of America Corp.
24. IBM
25. Marathon Petroleum
26. Cardinal Health
27. Boeing
28. Citigroup
29. Amazon.com
30. Wells Fargo
31. Microsoft
32. Proctor & Gamble
33. Home Depot
34. Archer Daniels Midland - None
35. Walgreens
36. Target
37. Johnson & Johnson
38. Anthem
39. MetLife
40. Google
41. State Farm Insurance Cos.
42. Freddie Mac
43. Comcast
44. PepsiCo
45. United Technologies
46. AIG
47. UPS
48. Dow Chemical
49. Aetna
50. Lowe's
51. ConocoPhillips
52. Intel
53. Energy Transfer Equity - None
54. Caterpillar
55. Prudential Financial
56. Pfizer
57. Disney
58. Humana
59. Enterprise Products Partners
60. Cisco Systems
61. Sysco
62. Ingram Micro
63. Coca-Cola
64. Lockheed Martin
65. FedEx
66. Johnson Controls
67. Plains GP Holdings - None
68. World Fuel Services - None
69. CHS
70. American Airlines Group
71. Merck
72. Best Buy
73. Delta Air Lines
74. Honeywell International
75. HCA Holdingsh - none
76. Goldman Sachs Group
77. Tesoro
78. Liberty Mutual Insurance Group
79. United Continental Holdings
80. New York Life Insurance
81. Oracle
82. Morgan Stanley
83. Tyson Foods
84. Safeway
85. Nationwide
86. Deere
87. DuPont
88. American Express
89. Allstate
90. Cigna
91. Mondelez International
92. TIAA-CREF
93. INTL FCStone
94. Massachusetts Mutual Life Insurance
95. DirecTV
96. Halliburton
97. Twenty-First Century Fox
98. 3M
99. Sears Holdings
100. General Dynamics - None

Fig. 5.3. Survey of Fortune 100 social-media usage

Some also include Google+ (pronounced "Google plus") and Tumblr. There are clear commonalities on which social-media platforms these companies use, with just a few outliers. Most interesting in evaluating this research is that Apple actually has no social media listed on its digital properties. It has accounts in all of these places but does not promote them on Apple's home pages or microsites or even from its mobile site. We checked its ad campaigns,

## Digital in the Boardroom

and it doesn't promote social media there, either. Consumers can find Apple on YouTube if they search within each platform, but they don't organically come across links to YouTube videos in Apple's owned spaces. Do you think they are on to something? Apple owns its digital space, and it is not directing consumers to other technology companies. Maybe that's the biggest lesson of all from this study. Costco was another one we found with no social media listed.

But, despite a couple of big companies abstaining from the trend, social media appears important. Will it always be? Some statistics suggest that it will. According to Social Media Today, global active Internet users now total 3.175 billion—half of the people on the planet. And active social-media users are 2.206 billion, or 30 percent of the planet. They also count 3.734 billion unique mobile users, accounting for more than half the people on the planet. Facebook claims half a million new users every day, with six new profiles every second.

While these are all impressive statistics, they also create questions about what these numbers really mean—which I'll cover more about in this chapter. And then there are many companies recognized as social-media experts. *Forbes* magazine cites Old Spice for using viral videos and Pizza Hut using Twitter to show humor. Staples answers customer questions via social media and provides humor about office life. Oreo uses social media to be quirky. During a Super Bowl blackout in 2013, Oreo tweeted a picture that said, "You can still dunk in the dark," showing how real-time social media can connect companies with consumers.

In the boardroom, it's important to ensure you at least have an understanding of the top social-media platforms and how they impact your company, as well as what you as an individual should and shouldn't be doing with them.

Let's take a look at what these platforms have come to mean to corporations and how the boardroom may want to think about social media as part of a holistic approach to digital:

**Facebook.** The original social-networking site, Facebook has turned friendship (at least in the digital sense) into a profitable business. Facebook builds out a timeline of your life for you and allows your friends to tag you in photos. Those photos, and anything else anyone says about you, can show up in your feed (and their feeds, and the feeds of others who were tagged with you). Do you have any "friends" who are converting old photos into digital images and tagging the people in them? Hope that you don't—or you'll see the 1970s version of yourself being commented upon by everyone you "friended."

Either the most beautiful or scariest part of Facebook is that the estimated 1.5 billion users are telecasting to marketers, advertisers, and Facebook everything about their lives—what they like and don't like, and often very deep and personal beliefs about politics, religion, and other topics that used to be reserved for private conversations. Some people are creating feeds and commenting on everything from how their manicures are that day to politics to their favorite shows. It's a dream come true for market researchers to have real-time feedback on the demographics they are targeting. Facebook enthusiasts willingly broadcast everything about themselves, which can in turn allow the site to tee up paid videos and advertising. Facebook can give politicians real-time feedback on what's trending and what's working well, and, as President Obama knows, deliver a platform to virally build support in an inexpensive and immediate way.

While Facebook has continually revised its privacy policies and promises of security, how secure can it ever be for someone who posts every detail of his or her life to hundreds, or sometimes thousands, of friends?

Facebook has been investing in patents that allow greater monetization of its platform by digging deeper into understanding what its users want before users even know what they want—and giving companies a way to tap into that. Facebook's patent filings suggest it is heavily focused on creating both privacy protection *and* targeted advertising based on social-networking activity.

Facebook provides a platform for people to share whatever they want about their lives and connect. Its monetizes that platform like a blend of a market-research agency and ad-distribution network, delivering messages, ads, and video to targeted groups with real-time feedback and the ability to track how people leave Facebook and where they go.

### Digital in the Boardroom

A company can use Facebook's purported billion users as an audience for photos, to start or respond to trends, and announce new products or sales to. Companies can create microsites inside Facebook with Facebook pages, where popularity can be tracked and proudly, or shamefully, posted for all to see. By advertising on Facebook, you can show up in the feeds of the type of people you want as consumers, whether it's a specific demographic or more niched toward people with specific likes or buying behavior.

Facebook will surely be tapping into third-party shopping in the near future. (How do I know? I find it in the patents they file.) Will Facebook span new generations or fade away like other fads? No one knows for sure, but most marketers want to have Facebook pages that in many ways mirror what they do on other social media. And pulling traffic from Facebook allows companies to better understand their targeted customers and reach them in a very personal way.

In the boardroom, you will want to know how your company is leveraging the data it can track and feedback it gets from Facebook. But this is just one piece of the social-media-data pie.

**Twitter.** Introduced in 2006, Twitter remains unprofitable, despite its 316 million user accounts. Plagued with fake accounts and people artificially driving up followers as a strategy, the platform is worshiped by celebrities and politicians whose tweets get read on the evening news. For celebrities wanting battles of wit, Twitter is an easy platform with its 140-character limit.

For the average user, once one starts following a few hundred publications, companies, or people, it's kind of hard to filter through the barrage of messages, even at 140 characters. Photos and videos embedded into the messaging, plus ads, create even more to wade through on a minute-by-minute basis. Check your Twitter feed at the end of the day, and there are probably hundreds of entries from just a few minutes ago—you'll never get through them all unless you have nothing else to do, which apparently is the case with some of the Twitterati, as many call them (the *Oxford Dictionaries* even have an entry for these frequent users of Twitter).

Software platforms like HubSpot or Hootsuite can help you manage all of this with a dashboard and track if someone mentions you in a tweet. This is helpful for companies to keep track of positive or negative comments about their products or services. Keeping up with Twitter has actually become a full-time job for dedicated social-media professionals hired to monitor and respond—often, a company has many of these on the payroll.

Twitter has been desperately trying to build a Facebook-like ad model or find ways to monetize the fire hose of information it collects from its users every day. Would the Kardashians pay for their Twitter accounts? Probably. But the real question is, would the other 316 million actual users pay? And, certainly, the reported 20 million, or one in every ten, fake accounts wouldn't pay. So, there's no subscriber model in the future for Twitter. Surely, pop culture won't allow Twitter to fail, so some economic model will undoubtedly emerge.

In the boardroom, Twitter should be seen as a source of information about your company's reputation, but taken through a lens that qualifies the voices. Are the comments from real customers? Is the data collected from Twitter statistically valid? Hashtags (#) are used to tag or filter for certain topics. This is how many companies build out trends—with a #like, #selfie, #newyearsday, #onthebeach, or endless other options. Tweeting with hashtags is a way to test if your company can create and sustain a trend or track a specific trend that starts up. If you want to know what's trending, go to Twitter's home page, where they list the top #trends. The average Twitter user tags photos or tweets with categories, and you can search or follow all tweets related to a certain category by using the hashtag as a search term. Twitter is a means for you to respond to unhappy customers and handle crises, but manage it carefully. It is another piece of the data puzzle because you can filter comments there and look for common themes or trends to provide real-time feedback. But run that through a lens of who your target customers are and how many of them are responding. The Twitterati send most of the messages, so it's important not to just look at numbers but to qualitatively ascertain the value of the information you are receiving.

**Instagram.** Instagram has become popular with millennials (who came of age around the year 2000) and the generation immediately following them (these don't have a formal nickname yet, but they were born after 2000 and are now becoming teenagers). The platform's functionality is simple and straightforward—loading photos and sharing them with people you know, and viewers can comment. It's less work than maintaining a Facebook page. Instagram focuses more on where you are and what you are doing versus commentary on anything and everything. Of course, Facebook bought Instagram for $20 billion to ensure that the new kid on the block didn't cannibalize its business. And, so far, it has remained true to the simple elegance of just posting pictures and a few comments.

The simplicity of Instagram makes it easy for companies to parallel posts on Twitter and Facebook. In fact, if you watch many companies, you'll see that their social-media posts are identical across platforms. There's not really as much data for a company to gather from Instagram other than whether hashtag trends you create or use are picked up. Or, if you create a contest or drive activity in some way, then you can easily measure it. One of the greatest value propositions for companies is that they can try to drive behavior digitally through Instagram, and the way people respond lets them know if it works or not, almost instantaneously.

**Pinterest.** Many companies also maintain Pinterest boards, particularly those that are more retail or consumer oriented. A simple way to post graphics and link to commerce sites, these online boards allow companies to create montages of images of interest to their customers, very much akin to the old-school pin board where people used to "pin up" photos they liked. As a user, you can search for almost anything, from DIY projects to holiday-gift ideas. It's a smorgasbord of photos and posts. It also lends insight into consumers' thinking.

For the user, Pinterest is a bit more creative than some other platforms. People tend to build boards on specific topics of interest, allowing observant companies to gain greater insight into how consumers interact with them. It's particularly popular for DIY projects, weddings, vacations, home design, and the like.

Pinterest is still struggling as well, as a start-up. Amazon pursued the new top-level domain dot-pin, so it remains to be seen if it will capitalize on the idea with more opportunities to create custom spaces. For example, Amazon could give Saks Fifth Avenue a saks.pin page in its top level domain dot-pin and Saks could then build out a digital pin board to share with its customers.

**Google+.** Google's sheer power forced it into the social scene a few years ago with Google+, which connects everything a user does in Google's universe into something that acts like a mash-up of all the other social media. While it's been slow to catch on, it's got the power of Google's data behind it. For most of the Fortune 100 companies we surveyed, what they post on Google+ mirrors what they do on Facebook. Because Google+ will ultimately tie into Google Play, Gmail, and every other facet of digital life in Google's Internet universe, in the long term, it could deliver something more compelling to the next generation.

Google's patent filings show it's inventing not just driverless cars, but also the smart home—from refrigerators and thermostats to door cameras and intelligence to run your home from anywhere. When all of that gets connected to Google+, privacy concerns get a lot bigger.

In the boardroom, the key thing to remember is that you probably already have a Google+ page, even if you don't realize it. As with all social media, be diligent about using privacy settings to limit what can be tagged or seen by others. At the corporate level, Google+ is one more place to aggregate data about you. Like all of digital, it's the putting all of these pieces together that matters.

**YouTube.** Google also owns YouTube. Most companies have YouTube channels. YouTube has become the second-biggest search engine after Google itself. It has the potential to create transformative change in the next generation. My thirteen-year-old doesn't spend any time on Facebook, and none of his friends have any desire to do that, but they do spend a lot of time on YouTube, watching videos, posting videos via text or on Instagram, and sharing what they find on YouTube.

YouTube has enough information that you could probably teach your children everything they need to know from kindergarten to twelfth grade if you wanted to put them in front of a computer all day. There are videos on everything from how to cook to how to take great photographs or fix a toilet. From the artistic to the mundane, someone has made a YouTube channel about it.

### Digital in the Boardroom

Celebrities are now created on YouTube. Bethany Mota went from being a teenager sharing how she was going to dress or style her hair that day, filming with an iPhone in her house, to a celebrity on *Dancing with the Stars* with fashion empires lining up to create lines of clothing or perfumes that she endorses.

YouTube is the biggest repository of video on the planet. Companies building out their YouTube channels can create longer-form, entertaining ads that could never air on traditional television. Companies can distribute content for free and build out loyal followers, intersecting with their posts on all other social media.

What's common among all of these social-media platforms is how companies market and consumers use the spaces. They're all very visual, driven by images, photos, and the ability to comment. Consumers love them because they can express themselves and become part of important discussions. These platforms all give individuals the ability to share in a one-to-many context what makes them who they are. Companies can get real-time feedback on what's working and what's not.

And it's not just about one platform or another. It's about the intersection of all of them. Like everything in digital, one piece is not the answer. It's how you use all of the pieces and create a digital world that gives your customers a better experience and in turn gives you valuable data and insights to drive your company forward to meet specific goals.

Then there's a different kind of social-media platform, one geared toward professionals and how they communicate with one another: **LinkedIn**. LinkedIn has become a social-networking site for professionals that began as an online résumé of sorts. Most people post their résumés there and maintain a sort of online Rolodex. To grow, however, LinkedIn continues to develop ways of leveraging the data it collects on its users, and it sells premium services to recruiters and salespeople.

Company boards should use LinkedIn cautiously. Do you need to be on LinkedIn? If so, be careful about only including what you want publicly disclosed about your work history. LinkedIn can serve as a nice digital Rolodex, but you need to carefully manage your privacy settings and only link to people you actually know. Most of the companies we surveyed generally mirror on LinkedIn much of what they do on Facebook or other social media.

**Other Social Media.** New social-media platforms are constantly emerging, like Vine, Tumblr, Periscope, and others, but I've provided for an overview of what we found to be most prevalently used among the Fortune 100.

**Hootsuite and HubSpot.** These social-media tools allow companies to post similar material across platforms from a single dashboard (though many social-media experts argue against simply replicating posts). If you just want to track your company in social media, a Hootsuite account lets you follow any mention of your company or your own personal name across platforms. You can bring your analyses of this information to board meetings.

If you are on a board, it's advisable to follow your company's mentions on social media and stay up to date on what your own people are putting out as well as what other companies or customers are saying about your company. You might be surprised by what you find.

You might also want to track your CEO or key senior management to know how they show up in social media. This will arm you with valuable intelligence and real-time understanding of how your company and its leadership are faring in the social-networking space. It can be very effective and easy to see it all in one navigation window. Hootsuite is free for up to three social profiles, and for just $9.99 a month, you could track up to fifty social profiles. A quick check of this dashboard once a week will keep you updated on what's happening in social media that directly impacts you.

## HOW DOES YOUR COMPANY MANAGE SOCIAL MEDIA?

So, now you have the basics about the most popular social-media sites in the Fortune 100—at least as of the beginning of 2016. The landscape changes so quickly, but it takes companies time to catch up. Whether you are an avid user of social media or afraid to join because they might start watching you (which they do), understanding social media is essential to leading your organization. The bigger questions for you as a board member are, how is your company managing the strategy, and how does the strategy connect to the rest of your digital strategy? In many companies, social media is just one step of a linear process to managing digital and may not be integrated cohesively into overall marketing plans. You can't just outsource your social strategy to a roomful of millennials; you must connect it to an overall, far-reaching digital strategy. As your company creates a digital world, consumers navigate in and out of social media, experiencing your digital company inside these platforms. It's not just how social media intersects with your SEO, e-commerce, or microsite strategies; it's how you integrate social-media information with other data that you can collect and aggregate.

An effective contemporary digital strategy is more cohesive and holistic, with information and analytics driving strategy in a connected way versus a linear decision-making process. The social piece has to be integrated with the others and driven by a deep understanding of what people want from you when they are on social-media platforms and how it intersects with their larger digital experience. It's the holistic digital-brand experience.

## SOCIAL AUTHORITY AND SEARCH

As the Internet has continued to evolve, search and social have started to intersect. New social sites have continually added to the complexity. Take a look at this graphic, and you can get a sense of how quickly new technology, social media, and apps are transforming the digital world.

It's no longer just about your SEO strategy online, but it's now also about what you do in social networks and in mobile (more on mobile in the next chapter). Social networking has created social authority, which current search algorithms take into account. Within social networks is the ability to become a clear authority. Whether it's about how to style your hair on a rainy day or how to take a photograph in the snow, authority is built in the social space.

Search algorithms have come to recognize social authority connecting to your digital spaces, so understanding the impact of social is a critical piece to how effective your company is in social media, as well as understanding what you should and shouldn't believe. How can you qualitatively evaluate the messenger on social media? The criteria to use are often contrary to what used to matter and are more about perception than reality. If I go on a safari, decide that I am now an expert on taking photos in Africa, and start posting such photos to social media, I shouldn't have the same credibility as a *National Geographic* photojournalist who has been taking pictures around the world his or her entire career.

But the interesting thing about social authority is that it has absolutely nothing to do with your "actual" credentials but rather how other people in the social networks view you. So, if I start posting pictures and tell how to take them and people follow me, link to me, and respond to me or mention me, then, according to search-engine algorithms, I will have more social authority than the expert photojournalist who doesn't use social media.

This is why companies that need to have authority or be the experts on certain subject matter must invest in smart and strategic social-media messaging to build social authority. If your company is trying to boost its status in search results, then it needs to determine its strategy, message, and voice. The social influence of your company comes from these key factors:

1. Knowing your topic and building authority
2. Engaging your community
3. Sharing useful content freely
4. Being consistent and useful
5. Marketing your strengths
6. Being a go-to resource
7. Being able to spot trends in data

In other words, you become a real authority for SEO when other people in the social sphere say you are. This may seem unfortunate or disheartening, but is the reality in a perception-oriented, 140-character-driven, social-media society.

Search continues to evolve in this space. Anything can be searched: a voice, picture, gesture, sound—anything. Bing and Google are building universal interfaces for search so that all facets of the human experience can be translated into the digital experience. Social search includes all forms of authority:

* Social blogs
* Pictures
* Internet forums
* Wikis
* Videos
* Microblogs
* Social bookmarks
* Podcasts
* Weblogs
* Ratings
* RSS feeds

As I've been saying, many companies replicate content across social media, but given search-algorithm behavior, I recommend a few corporate social-media do's and don'ts for building social authority and credibility:

## DO

1. Repurpose only relevant content.
2. Consider the platform and audience.
3. Offer the same customer services online and offline.
4. Ensure a helpful response in a short span of time.
5. Give a story line to videos.
6. Line up your video marketing with your overall campaign.
7. Use platforms like Instagram and Vine, not just YouTube.
8. Create an interesting story line around your products or services.
9. Invite stories on customer experiences.

10. Use ads only in sync with your overall social-media strategy.
11. Provide regular updates.
12. Encourage customer engagement.
13. Add custom descriptions of photos or pins.

## DON'T

1. Copy and paste the same content from one platform to the next.
2. Mix advertising and customer service.
3. Neglect negative comments.
4. Forget to incorporate customer feedback.
5. Add too many annotations to videos.
6. Create videos that are too long.
7. Focus only on your brand rather than what's relevant to the audience.
8. Create cliché story lines that others have already used.
9. Sell products directly in your content.
10. Forget to promote across platforms.

As you begin to evaluate your company's approach to social media, keep in mind that social is constantly changing and new platforms will continue to emerge. The key is how to leverage and use the data, drive behavior, and build real authority in the important social spaces.

## SOCIAL MEDIA AND YOU

Your communications and legal departments have likely rolled out some type of social-media policy for employees, but you should also consider if the board and senior management should have their own policy on social media. I touched on this in chapter 3 when I talked about cybersecurity and how to protect yourself and senior managers. It's imperative to keep in mind that when you, the CEO, or C-suite executives participate in social media, you could be viewed as official spokespersons of your company. How do you control that to ensure that you and your fellow board members don't inadvertently start a Twitter war or social-media battle? You absolutely must have a policy to control what your fellow board members, CEO, and senior executives do and say in social media. It's about security and control in an age where things can get out of control in seconds.

In years past, consultants have popped up to train sales reps and executives on how to communicate in this 140-character-driven society and how to use all of this social media. They run roadshows to get everyone excited and engaged in these new platforms, extolling the virtues of short, concise messages with photos instead of words for people who no longer can pay attention for more than seven seconds. One would assume that if you've made it to a senior position in a company or serve on a board of directors, you not only can read, but you can pay attention for more than seven seconds. It's frightening and dangerous to think that we now have a society of people who don't have the diligence to read or think but rather react hysterically or emotionally in social media without first gathering objective information and building an informed opinion—but that is, in fact, exactly what social media has created.

The hysteria becomes viral, and we end up with a lot of misinformed people. Social media has done a lot of good things, too, in creating connections that couldn't exist before, but as a board member or senior executive, you don't need to be trained to use social media like the kids do. You need to be trained how to use it as someone who is responsible for a lot of people and that what you do and say in social media can have immediate, profound, and far-reaching consequences. The genie is out of the bottle, and it's not going back in, so there's not much point in debating the cost-benefit to our society of the social-media age. It's only going to evolve. While many may feel like their personal accounts are theirs to use as they see fit, the reality is that social media just doesn't work that way. In a boardroom, you may be able to discern the difference between someone speaking on his or her own behalf versus on that of the company, but not everyone else out there in the world can. They will take what you say and do and manipulate it to meet whatever their social, political, or economic agendas need from you. You may think you are under the radar and that no one cares—until someone does. Then your digital fingerprints are out there for everyone to find.

Donald Trump, during his run for the White House, famously snarks back at critics on Twitter. While this approach seemingly has worked for him for a while, it doesn't work for most people.

## THE FUTURE OF SOCIAL MEDIA

Desperate for attention, the most vulnerable members of our society—the young, the insecure, the lonely, and the disenfranchised—have willingly given away their privacy to anyone willing to like them and follow them in social media.

It's provided a platform for the best and worst of humanity in real time around the globe. It reveals the best in us when we provide love, support, and encouragement when people need it most, even from strangers who can suddenly feel connected to us through the social-media phenomenon. This is its upside.

But, it shows our worst when we encourage violence and hatred and provide solidarity for those who feel most alone and ready to blame others for their problems and misfortune and angry enough to do more than just cyberbully them. Unfortunately, the worst in us can easily turn into real violence. In America, it's the mentally unstable championed by social media and lifelike video games and virtual reality that have given rise to very real violent acts in our schools, churches, and communities. Around the world, terrorist organizations like ISIS have used social media to recruit and galvanize those who will kill themselves and everyone around them in their hatred of others.

If there's one thing we can all know with certainty, it's that technology and the way we live will continue to change. Social media is no different. Since the dawn of social media with Facebook, we have seen social spaces come and go and others pop up and survive.

It's likely that the next big thing in social media is just being developed by a teenager as an idea to solve a problem that many of us don't even realize is a problem. That's the nature of digital, and the only fair assumption is that it will continue to change. For boards, the key is to get trained on contemporary social media, cybersecurity, and privacy issues and set clear policies that hold this assumption and that privacy will continue to erode in favor of convenience and connectivity.

Your senior managers should have a fresh look at the digital world and particularly social media. They need a holistic plan and strategy that integrates all facets of the digital world and leverages the fact that you can drive behavior or test theories in social media and get instantaneous results. That's very powerful, but only if it's integrated across the digital strategy of the organization. On our digital map, social media is just one piece to consider. We'll continue to work our way around the map. But the key is that the strategy is holistic and not siloed. Silos allow the status quo to prevent your company from spotting important trends or ensure that old assumptions or paradigms drive decision-making—to your peril.

## KEY TAKEAWAYS FROM CHAPTER 5

* Compare your company's social-media usage to that on the Fortune 100's chart in this chapter. Should you consider an approach like that of Apple or Costco and strip away other companies' logos from your home page and own your own digital spaces fully?
* Use Hootsuite or something similar to track how you, your colleagues, and your company are mentioned and discussed in social media. This is important data to share in board meetings.
* Carefully manage and continually develop social-media policies for you and your fellow board members, C-suite executives, and key personnel in the organization. Get training or support if you need more information on how to manage your privacy in social media.
* Social media is all about perceptions, not reality. Understand this fully before you dive in—and if you do, manage that perception carefully.

*Chapter 6*

## MOBILE, APPS, AND THE INTERNET OF THINGS

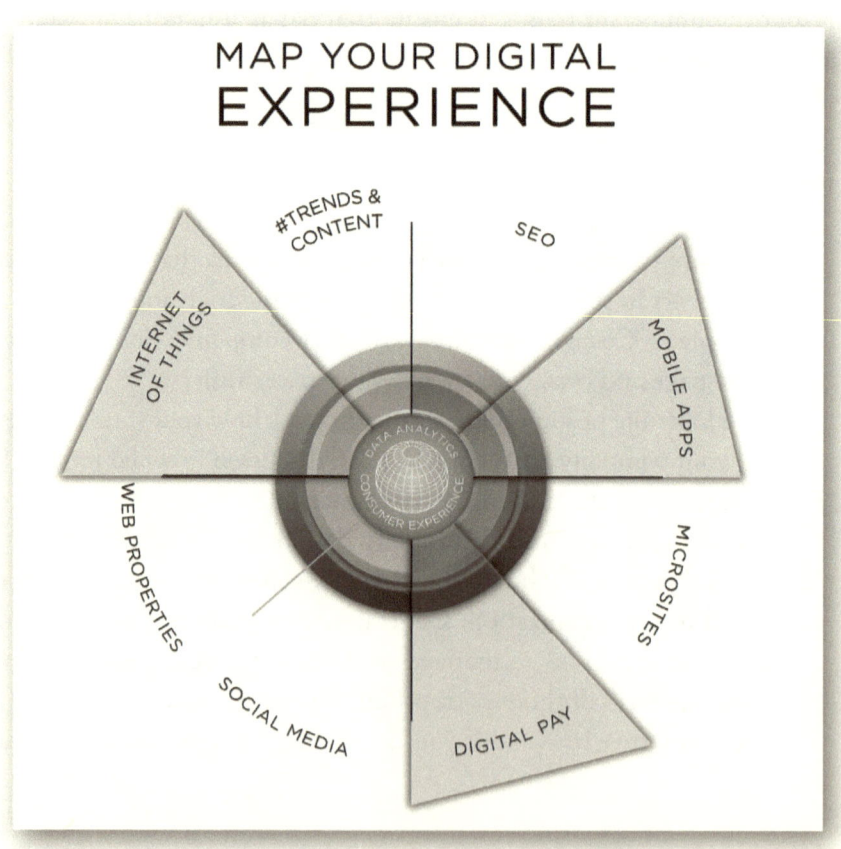

Fig. 6.1. Digital map of mobile and the Internet of things

### Digital in the Boardroom

As we continue around the map of your company's digital world, we come to mobile, apps, the Internet of things, and digital pay—we are reaching a point where the digital world truly interfaces with our real world through devices and technology.

Our mobile, on-the-go digital experiences are driven by better and better devices, and soon, the Internet of things will further transform our lives. We all experience the ability to seamlessly weave in and out of our digital worlds with devices that are now more than just phones or tablets or laptops that we carry around, but are wearables like glasses and watches. They are so powerful now that we can load several movies on any one of these small devices. We can make restaurant reservations, change our flights or seats on a flight, download movies, and hail cabs all with the touch of a screen. Any downtime is now filled with tapping away on our phones that directly take us to the specific functions, information, or experiences we seek. All this translates into a shift in mobile—on-the-go behavior that impacts how you experience your digital world.

The idea of apps changes search and navigation of the Internet, and we'll take a look at that and what it means for optimizing your digital world. But it has also changed the expectations we have about how we want to engage the Internet from our devices or things. We need apps to make it fast and easy. But, at a certain point, we can only manage so many apps, and we reach a point of diminishing return. So, what does that mean for the future? This is an important question.

So, also, are these: As a board member, do you know who is responsible for your mobile experience? Who is thinking about how the Internet of things will change your company and what new technologies you may need in the future to respond to this new way of living? The new connectivity impacts consumers all over the planet; how will it impact your customers? Whether you serve another business or the individual consumer, this technology will impact all. Will it create new competitors that didn't exist before?

For example, if your company is in the retail space, will devices in the home or apps keep track of purchases so that consumers can curate their closets or the design of their homes? Smart refrigerators and devices will soon keep track of what's in consumer kitchens, to help them not just make their grocery lists, but also manage recipes and ingredients, find coupons, and pay for it all without the touch of a screen.

And what happens to your privacy when you allow all of those apps you use to know where you are all the time? This is an important consideration for board members. Are you walking around with sensitive documents? How will these new innovations change the marketplace of today, and how will you be ready? These are the signals you need to look for so you don't get blindsided.

## SEARCH AND MOBILE

Many have predicted that apps will soon replace search because they offer simple ways to do exactly what people want. If you want to change your seat on an airplane or rebook your flight, the airline's app is easier to use than going to a search engine or sometimes even the airline's desktop home page. If you want to make dinner reservations, OpenTable makes it so easy to find a reservation, make it, and add it to your calendar while inviting your guests. The app from your rental-car company can tell you which car is ready for you and where to pick it up. For the young and single, Tinder helps them meet people in their areas. Pandora, Facebook, Twitter, eBay, Nordstrom, Macy's, and nearly 91 percent of other top brands all have apps that allow you to listen to music, read your social feed, and buy whatever you want.

Even among business-to-business companies, nearly two-thirds have built apps. Once your information is stored, payment and delivery are all just a touch screen away. If you know what you want, using apps makes life on the go much easier than messing around with a search engine and looking through lists of links or arduously navigating crowded home pages with too much irrelevant information. But do we reach a point of diminishing returns? How many apps on your device is too many? A hundred? Five hundred? A thousand?

According to Mashable, the average smartphone user has twenty-six apps installed. Unless your company makes that cut, most consumers won't use your app. Most of us get rid of apps we don't use that just take up space and

## Digital in the Boardroom

drain our device's power. We declutter our digital lives just like we declutter our homes. There's no question, then: for companies, the key is to really understand your customers and know what they need so that your app delivers such a great service and value to them that they wouldn't dare live without it.

And, you have to think about how apps transcend devices. Phones and tablets have specific functions versus what you might want your Internet TV to do. On your Internet TV, you likely want more content and channels, as well as apps that help you navigate them or your shopping experience. You're only going to have so many apps on your screen without feeling overwhelmed and wanting some order to it.

For example, you might not set up an app for every single television network, but you might install one that gives you access across your favorite channels. On the other hand, if you shop at a specific store frequently, you might download its app. Your grocery store, for example, might have an app you use more regularly than, say, that of a boutique you only visit once a year.

If your company's app isn't in a customer's top twenty-six, they still need to be able to find you digitally when searching from a device or thing. We know that searching on a mobile device is more difficult than on a laptop or desktop computer with a full-size keyboard. Typing on smaller devices is harder, and we can only see so many search results at a time.

Google has responded to all of this by ensuring its algorithms consider GPS location to deliver geolocation-relevant search results. Undoubtedly, search will continue to get better. This is why you must look at the digital experience holistically. If you just focus on the app or one component of the digital experience, then you miss how you are going to bring people from one space to the next to grow your business.

To put all this in perspective, in 1999, Nokia released to the public the first cell phone with Internet capabilities. It was the Nokia 7110. Fifteen years later, 1.3 million apps are available in the Google Play store, and 1.2 million are available in Apple's App Store. The App Store started on July 21, 2008, with nine hundred apps available. A year later, it had sixty-five thousand. On May 3, 2010, it had two hundred thousand apps. It had half a million by October 4, 2011, and in 2012, over six hundred thousand.

The Google Play store started in December of 2009 with sixteen thousand apps. By October 2010, it had a hundred thousand. In October 2012, it had seven hundred thousand. It now has over 1.3 million, surpassing the Apple App Store for the first time. The statistics prove that apps have grown in popularity.

When it comes to how people use apps, it's not surprising that use of the clock app peaks at night, when users set their alarms, or that calendar usage peaks in the morning and at lunchtime, when people plan out their days. Facebook usage rises throughout the day, getting a boost when people are back home in the afternoon. Google Maps peaks during end-of-day rush hour. Weather-app usage peaks in the morning and evening, and finance apps rise in the morning and taper toward the end of the workday as markets close. Productivity apps rise early in the morning and drop through the evening. Media and video use goes up steadily throughout the day.

None of this is exactly surprising. But what is relevant is that it's all being done on mobile devices—phone or tablet and, soon, wearables, Internet TVs, and things around our houses and our lives. As the Internet of things takes over, usage will continue into the evening hours.

We know that smartphones have transformed our lives, but the next evolution from smartphones is the Internet of things. Smart everything, as it may turn out, will run alongside the dot-anything Internet space. It's not hard to imagine a world where our home refrigerator apps tell us we're out of milk before we leave the office along with a suggestion for what to cook for dinner with what we still have in there. Our houses will automatically turn on the home alarm system when everyone is home safely or everyone leaves for the day, and the TV will have our favorite shows or movies lined up and ready to play. And, as we move from couches to our bedrooms, it will simply pick up again there. Facebook is building virtual reality to connect to our mobile devices with its Oculus headset, which will further the Internet-of-things approach to life.

Companies that fail to react to change typically are not around much longer. Blockbuster failed to evolve, whereas Netflix adapted to a digital model. That one may seem obvious, but the current digital changes impact every company, not just media companies. In the boardroom, you need to push against assumptions and recognize that things will change dramatically. You need to ensure that your executives are not living in a status-quo society that downplays the risk of change and insists that everything will always stay the same. The Internet will connect all of these things. Apps and app-like functions will continue to be a driver, but underneath it all remains a web of landing pages, home pages, or microsites that may be mobile or Internet-of-things enabled.

Fitbit can track everything you eat and do, and Google, Facebook, Apple, Amazon, Adobe, and so many more will be there to track everything else and tee up ads that relate to your life.

In the future, devices and things will track your every movement and even bio signs to know *how* you are doing. While it creates tremendous convenience for helping us throughout our day (I'm sure we will someday ask how we figured out what to have for dinner without a smart something making a suggestion), the inevitable question is, what does this do to our privacy? Particularly when you consider all of the money going into all of this invention, you realize that it has to be paid for somehow: either we're buying things, or these companies are selling our privacy.

## GLOBAL LAW AND HOW IT IMPACTS MOBILE AND THE INTERNET OF THINGS

The global laws on privacy are vast and deep and beyond the scope of this book. But they are worth mentioning when discussing how all the data your company gathers from mobile devices and digital pay impacts compliance with privacy laws. Privacy laws vary from country to country. In much of Europe, privacy is given a heightened level of protection. However, in other countries, like China, Russia, North Korea, and many Middle Eastern countries, the consumer can assume that all digital activity is being monitored, as the Internet itself is censored and policed in many of these territories. The United States also has many privacy laws that bear steep penalties if personally identifiable information is exposed. These differences in policy by country will not likely recede but expand in the years to come. If the differences continued, we could end up with internet isolationism in the digital age, meaning it's no longer one world wide web, but rather a network of each country setting its own rules and policies to govern its citizens and their access to information on the internet. Eric Schmidt warns, "The next stage in this process...will be collective editing, states forming communities of interest to edit the web together, based on shared values or geopolitics. Collective action—be it in the physical or virtual world—will be a logical move for many states that find they lack the resources, the reach, or the capability to influence vast territories."

As you consider how our devices will connect every facet of our lives to the Internet, do not forget that the Internet has to be maintained, and so do the policies that govern it. Your company must take a role in how those policies are set or face the peril of reacting to policies created by others. I briefly mentioned in chapter 2 the role of ICANN. Your company needs to send someone there to really understand it. Whether it's an executive or a lobbyist you hire to represent you, someone needs to report back to you, the board, and senior management on what's happening with Internet policy and how it could impact you. Do you think cybersecurity and these issues are not related? It's all connected and all related. That's how the digital world works.

## DYNAMICALLY CHANGING AND PREDICTING THE FUTURE WITH THE INTERNET OF THINGS

A chapter on mobile, apps, and the Internet of things can't conclude without touching on a critical issue—how fast and dynamically mobile strategies will change. The mobile category is changing so fast that even the best chief marketing officers can hardly keep up with it. In early 2016, messaging apps like Viber, Line, Snapchat, Groupme, Kik, and so many others had come online and may take off and then fall again, get acquired, or merge into something else. There are countless new apps every day. In the C-suite or the boardroom, you can hardly be expected to keep up with all of them, but what's important is to look for the signals that indicate big change is coming so your company is prepared and doesn't fall behind.

There are many sources for predicting the future. Eric Schmidt offered his predictions for the future of digital, which were not unlike those of a 2014

## Digital in the Boardroom

Outlook article from *The Futurist* magazine. He predicts how devices and Internet of things will transform our lives, from waking us with the scent of coffee or cinnamon rolls to helping us plan our drives to work to avoid traffic—a just-in-time management philosophy to maximize every moment of our days. Smartphones and apps will help us diagnose health problems and optimize our workouts. But, as all of this is happening, an Accenture study shows that digital cannot be considered in isolation and that most companies are struggling because the real-world, physical life where we still actually interact with one another in brick-and-mortar locations is often run completely separately from digital. And today, they must intersect. All facets of digital and the physical world must create—together—the best possible experience to maintain consumer trust and interest.

Like all facets of digital, your strategy requires a holistic approach to intersect it with the overall digital experience so that you can understand what could be coming in the future and be prepared for a whole new world. When these types of paradigm shifts occur, every business has to evolve. How will consumers consume your products or services in the future? How will they navigate across the digital map of your company, and where will you integrate with their lives? And how will your organization manage the changing laws and policies in a global Internet divided by differing geopolitical beliefs and privacy expectations? In chapter 9, I'll focus on how to manage digital and provide a best practice for what you may want to consider in the future.

If you want to get a real sense of the future of mobile, apps, and the Internet of things and what companies may launch, look no further than patent filings. In a highly device- and app-driven space, the need to protect the investment made in development is essential. That's why we see filings and activity so heavily focused on devices, apps, social understanding, and the Internet of things. We've provided a bit about patent filings from our own research, but I also include here a summary from *Intellectual Asset Management* (*IAM*) magazine, the premier global intellectual-property magazine.

The *IAM* survey provides a snapshot of how many patents, and in what categories, big technology companies are developing related to mobile and the Internet of things (see Figure 6.2). Board members need to understand these trends because they provide important signals about the future, particularly with mobile and the Internet of things transforming lives and businesses.

According to *IAM*, patents are now being filed for the following:

* Devices or things that you physically touch and use
* Networks that connect the things and the apps
* Big-data functions that analyze, crunch, and do something with information
* Apps that deliver the interface and the service
* Rules and analytics engines that crunch it all together
* Databases that hold it all
* Security that helps ensure that information you provide is authenticated and real, even if its biometric
* Functions that integrate external information from other sources, such as weather or traffic
* Integrations with other business systems such as reservations, ticketing, or invoicing and e-payment

Most heavily, we see wearables, but that, too, is shifting.

My company monitors patent filings by big technology drivers to look for trends. We see big trends in the Internet of things and how we as individuals interact with those things:

* Gesture-based technology in mobile and devices or mobile apps are being filed by powerhouse companies like Amazon, Apple, Google, Facebook, Adobe, Intel, and others
* Big telecom companies like Comcast, Charter, and Verizon are investing in video on demand, Internet-based pay TV, electronic coupons, and network security systems to manage traffic
* Big tech companies are filing patents to better stream content, deliver ads, and calculate ad fees
* Companies like Intel are developing technology for managing media content and broadcast distribution

# Digital in the Boardroom

| Portfolio | IoT wearable patents | Sensor patents | Sensor system patents | Power patents | Processor patents | Wireless patents | Product feature patents | % of total corporate portfolio |
|---|---|---|---|---|---|---|---|---|
| Microsoft | 962 | 89 | 407 | 71 | 287 | 38 | 170 | 3% |
| Google | 914 | 109 | 409 | 99 | 103 | 59 | 277 | 4% |
| Apple | 858 | 210 | 483 | 45 | 159 | 15 | 42 | 5% |
| Qualcomm | 752 | 173 | 359 | 209 | 62 | 44 | 57 | 3% |
| Medtronic | 655 | 14 | 516 | 38 | 11 | 39 | 77 | 4% |
| Philips | 596 | 17 | 425 | 32 | 31 | 38 | 83 | 5% |
| IBM | 571 | 43 | 243 | 48 | 137 | 44 | 73 | 1% |
| Cardiac pacemakers | 486 | 2 | 468 | 12 | 1 | 9 | 7 | 19% |
| Intel | 475 | 70 | 224 | 128 | 40 | 48 | 32 | 2% |
| Nokia /Alcatel-Lucent | 463 | 36 | 186 | 91 | 62 | 66 | 53 | 2% |
| Seiko | 455 | 180 | 99 | 105 | 1 | 0 | 76 | 2% |
| BlackBerry | 403 | 74 | 246 | 68 | 20 | 32 | 16 | 4% |
| Samsung | 400 | 55 | 98 | 157 | 23 | 19 | 55 | 1% |
| Panasonic | 360 | 61 | 105 | 132 | 28 | 3 | 34 | 1% |
| Siemens | 341 | 28 | 187 | 57 | 34 | 17 | 23 | 1% |
| Nike | 308 | 24 | 175 | 4 | 3 | 1 | 154 | 7% |
| AT&T | 287 | 12 | 74 | 14 | 77 | 74 | 47 | 2% |
| LG Electronics | 275 | 41 | 53 | 56 | 40 | 40 | 52 | 1% |
| Sony | 268 | 29 | 109 | 44 | 48 | 4 | 39 | 1% |
| Canon | 241 | 17 | 118 | 55 | 27 | 1 | 24 | 1% |
| Motorola | 199 | 39 | 87 | 31 | 5 | 22 | 36 | 5% |
| Toshiba | 182 | 11 | 78 | 59 | 19 | 4 | 12 | 1% |
| Gentex | 137 | 57 | 92 | 0 | 1 | 1 | 0 | 21% |
| Lenovo | 135 | 27 | 52 | 33 | 15 | 4 | 9 | 3% |
| Verizon | 113 | 7 | 32 | 8 | 30 | 32 | 11 | 2% |
| NEC | 109 | 6 | 40 | 45 | 7 | 0 | 13 | 1% |
| FitBit | 94 | 3 | 82 | 0 | 2 | 0 | 25 | 60% |
| Nintendo | 92 | 20 | 71 | 0 | 3 | 1 | 1 | 5% |
| Immersion | 87 | 22 | 50 | 2 | 10 | 1 | 24 | 14% |
| Garmin | 83 | 12 | 30 | 0 | 3 | 37 | 10 | 14% |
| Polar | 69 | 0 | 58 | 0 | 2 | 1 | 15 | 45% |
| Casio | 58 | 6 | 27 | 4 | 1 | 0 | 21 | 2% |
| Citizen_Holdings | 56 | 11 | 5 | 13 | 0 | 0 | 28 | 6% |
| Oracle | 46 | 16 | 13 | 4 | 10 | 1 | 2 | 0% |
| Plantronics | 12 | 1 | 4 | 0 | 0 | 1 | 8 | 3% |

Fig. 6.2. Internet-of-things patent portfolio

* Motorola is developing wearables
* Adobe is developing technology for streaming video across social networks and devices alongside digital rights management and digital pay technology

We know that Facebook bought Oculus, and they now develop virtual-reality technology. Google has patents filed on everything from thermostats and refrigerators to smart front doors for your home, truly building the smart home. When it's all connected to the Internet and Google tailors search to your needs, do you think it might have something of value to every advertiser? Talk about market research! Of course, Google connects driverless cars and contact lenses connected to the Internet, so Iron Man technology may not be that far away.

Google's patents, in particular are telling. They have filed them for the following:

* Automated handling of a package delivery at a smart home
* Detecting driving with a wearable computing device
* Determining user gestures for dismissing electronic notifications
* A digital photo frame
* Efficient communication devices for a home network
* Electronic-device housing and assembly
* Handling specific visitor behavior at an entryway to a smart home
* Handling visitor interaction at a smart home in a "do not disturb" mode
* Initially detecting a visitor at a smart home
* Interacting with a detected visitor at an entryway to a smart home (this one was fast-tracked)
* Leveraging neighborhoods to handle potential visitors at a smart home
* Occupant notification of visitor interaction with a doorbell at a smart home
* Routing optimization for package delivery to a smart home
* Smart-home control system providing HVAC-system-dependent responses to hazard-detection events
* Smart-home hazard detector with adaptive, heads-up prealarm criteria
* Smart-home system that facilitates monitoring carbon-monoxide levels
* Visitor feedback to visitor interaction with a doorbell at a smart home

This technology is being developed, and if something is important to your company, you can track patent activity to understand and predict what may be coming in the Internet of things and how it may affect you. Whether you sell technology or soap, how consumers live in this new world will impact how your products are bought and consumed in the future.

The future of life with the Internet of everything? It's not hard to imagine what a day in the life of a senior executive might look like and how every facet of it will be tracked by a device connected to the Internet.

## A MORNING IN THE NEAR FUTURE

You'll awaken to an alarm connected to a body sensor set to go off after you complete a REM cycle so that you feel fully rested and don't need to keep hitting a snooze button. You'll have set that alarm to trigger something that is pleasant to you, whether it's the smell of pancakes, eggs, and bacon or just fresh lilac. Perhaps the sound of a stream or the ocean would be nice, or maybe you long for just the white-noise sounds of the city. Whatever pleases your senses can all be preprogrammed into your device. Your device could be a phone, something that looks like an alarm clock, or a panel on the wall in your bedroom. Your bed and biosensor will all be connected, providing you the best possible night's sleep.

If you're having any health problems, your biosensor will alert you to any problems you should address. Your biosensors will also help you make good nutritional choices, alerting you to any deficiencies in your body so you can eat the right foods and take the right vitamin supplements that morning.

All the while, your devices will be connected to your calendar and the other people in your house so that you are alerted to any potential traffic or commuting delays for not just you, but also your spouse, your kids, or any planned activity. If you are traveling that day, information you need about your trip will be presented to you just in time. Of course, your coffee, tea, or whatever is your beverage of choice will be ready for you, and your refrigerator will apprise you of what foods need to be eaten or purchased.

As you consume your breakfast, you can decide what to have for dinner, and your smart refrigerator and kitchen will tell your other smart devices what you need later in the day or possibly even recommend an order from the local grocery-delivery company for it to be there in time for you to make dinner that night.

Your devices will alert each family member when he or she needs to leave the house so that they all arrive exactly on time, because your devices will be connected to everything happening in the external world. You may get to work by driverless car in the future or perhaps a car that requires a lot less of you so you can read the paper or catch up on e-mails while listening to music or news that you like.

By the time you've arrived at work, you're rested, have had a stress-free commute, and are ready to face the day.

Sounds amazing, right? Surely there will be some glitches in all this, and one can only imagine if the Internet goes down what happens to this utopia, let alone if someone hacks into it.

## WHAT'S NEXT?

There's no question that mobile, apps, and the Internet of things will make our lives easier. They will help us optimize our bodies for nutrition and health, get better sleep, plan our days, and take care of mundane tasks with a quick order to Siri or whomever else is invented to live inside these devices as our fictional butlers or personal assistants. Now we can all live like the rich and famous.

All the while, the only way all of this technology can work is if you give yourself to the matrix—the Internet. You must release all of your personal and private data out into the vast universe of cyberspace, trusting the companies that create the tools and devices to safeguard your privacy. While they file patents to crunch numbers and create algorithms to deliver all of this just-in-time personal service, we know that the only way they can make their vision a reality is by capturing and crunching data about not just ourselves, but everyone else. And the data about others influences the data about you.

Big technology companies are already trying to figure out how to discern when more than one person in a household is using a shared account. You may be interested in very different content than are your children or your spouse. You may buy different products. But in the interest of streamlining accounts, if you all share, do the lines blur?

And if Uber can track when you request a car and where you go anywhere on the planet, what will Google know when it tracks what's in your refrigerator and what food and beverages you consume every day? If Apple's fit devices can tell you when you've have too much of something, is that good or bad? What if companies tie insurance coverage or bonuses to how healthy you appear in the data?

That's where the questions come in. What if your smart bed confuses you and your spouse and provides a misdiagnosis? Or what if there is a malfunction and you take the wrong vitamins or medication or head out at the wrong time? What if those fit devices miscalculate and the consequences are serious? Certainly, the possibility for something to glitch is there. Before most consumers even know about these problems, there are teams of people working to solve them and file patents on them—that's how we can know that work is being done toward this future and how we can make predictions about it.

In the boardroom, you don't have to have all the answers, but you do need to fully understand the reality of mobile and the Internet of things and how your company connects the dots. You also want to be aware of your own personal choices and how they can impact your privacy.

Even if you are not in the technology business, this technology will transform your life and that of everyone around you. As we move toward the future, there's one thing we all know will never change—our desire for great content.

## KEY TAKEAWAYS FROM CHAPTER 6

* The Internet of things will transform all of our lives. Every company will be impacted by it. Understanding the trajectory of mobile, apps, and the Internet of things is an important function at the board level to ensure the company is on a strategic path of strength.
* We can predict some of this by tracking new patents and big mergers or acquisitions of technology to identify who may be doing what in the future.
* Global privacy laws will impact everything your company does in its digital world. The cost of making a mistake or doing business in

some regions could become too high. Understanding these risks is also critical to avoiding a devastating oversight blunder.

* Mobile and the Internet of things must connect to all other facets of your digital world if you want to fully protect yourself and leverage future opportunities.

*Chapter 7*

# EVERYTHING WILL CHANGE, BUT GOOD CONTENT WILL ALWAYS BE KING

When Google released its Hummingbird algorithm in September of 2013, it initially caused widespread panic across the SEO community because largely, it meant the keyword era was over and that search would behave more like people do (i.e., the better the content, the higher the ranking of a web page). For marketers with good content, this was a good thing, but for those relying on old SEO strategies and using skimpy or repeated content with an emphasis on keywords, with Hummingbird in charge of quality control, the cost to drive eyeballs to a web page might have gone up.

Hummingbird would look for content that was good, dynamic, and related to what the searcher was seeking—like a human researcher might do. At that same time, we also learned that companies like Amazon, Intel, Netflix, and Verizon had all started to invest in original programming, recognizing the old adage, "Content is king." These tech companies all recognized that the future will reward entities that produce good content that people want, regardless of how many keywords are used. This is very disruptive and a change in long-standing Internet business models.

Flashback to 1994 and a speech by Ed Artz, then CEO of Procter & Gamble, where he predicted this trend. He warned that ad-supported media could be in trouble. He said, "If advertising is no longer needed to pay most of the cost of home entertainment, then advertisers like us will have a hard time achieving the reach and frequency we need." In the current age of media via technology, it's easy to look back and see that he was right. He predicted that people would become more programming driven and less channel driven. His warning was largely unheard by marketing managers at the time—much like today's marketing managers are largely ignoring some of the coming changes, protecting their silos, budgets, and agendas.

What Ed Artz recognized before *digital* was even a term was that, regardless of when, where, how, or with what people access content, advertisers and companies need good content to connect with consumers.

We now know that devices will change, software will change, and the very way we live our lives in the digital world will change. But what will not change is our desire as humans to be entertained. The type of content may change, of course, but we will all long for good content, however we define it. For all companies, this means we have to understand our roles in the content chain. Do we create it, support it, distribute it, or some combination of the above?

Week after week, articles about how big tech companies are investing in content and consumers are cutting the cable cords are covered, not just in digital media but in mainstream publications as well. In the *Wall Street Journal* on September 23, 2015, Miriam Gottfried quoted T-Mobile chief John Legere at an investor conference: "What's happening in the world is all content is going to be Internet and all Internet will be viewed on mobile devices. That is all you need to know to understand that it's going to happen from Disney to Comcast to Verizon to T-Mobile." This reality that all content will be digital and delivered from some type of Internet-connected device or thing is widely accepted now. The need for good content will never go away.

Couple this with Google's continued YouTube channel growth and its Hummingbird algorithm focused on quality content, and it's easy to see that every company, at some point, is going to get into the content business to promote its products and services. But the concept of creating programming and content that tie to selling products is not exactly new.

The original soap operas started on radio in 1933 and on television in the 1950s, largely supported by soap company Procter & Gamble. These dramatic programs were created to capture the hearts of American housewives at home taking care of laundry, cleaning, cooking, and the like. Remember the phrase, "Brought to you by Ivory"? That was the idea. Create content that appeals to your target audience to promote your product. These dramatic programs were sponsored by soap companies who wanted women to get hooked on shows and love the characters so much that they would tune in day after day or week after week and, as a result, buy the products that sponsored them.

As time went on, daytime soap operas continued to capture viewership, from teens and college students (a coveted market today) to stay-at-home moms. New dramatic series emerged and continued for decades, from *As the World Turns* to *All My Children*. For you die-hard *General Hospital* (*GH*) fans, who wouldn't love tuning in to John Stamos or Rick Springfield day after day? But there's more to this than just a little soap-opera trivia. The point is that the very concept of creating content to sell products has been at the heart and soul of television and the entertainment industry for the last sixty years.

But now, everyone can produce content. In chapter 5, I mentioned Bethany Mota, the teen sensation who has built a subscriber base in the millions for her down-to-earth, practical teenage-beauty tips. From a six-figure income via its ads to endorsement deals, new celebrities and businesses are formed every day on YouTube. The cost of equipment needed to create content has become so low that, with some talent, it's not difficult to produce quality content. So why are big tech companies pushing so hard on the content front? Should that be an indicator for other companies to do the same? Does it matter that many of the big tech companies building content will also soon launch their channels of the Internet with new top-level domains (i.e., Google, Amazon, Netflix, Microsoft)?

The big tech companies recognize that eyeballs and wallets will follow the latest and greatest story lines and characters that appeal to them—the soap-opera idea. They built empires on the "if you build it, they will come" approach to everything that works in the digital world. They get that content is the future. Put out great content, and the people flock to your digital world to watch it. It can be supported directly or by ads from companies like Procter & Gamble. And for Google, Amazon, and Netflix, they will soon have their own channels of the Internet platform as the backbones to their digital worlds. So the more important question becomes, will they use the content to sell their products, or will the content become the product?

Some of the best ads now air only on YouTube or online. Remember the Toyota "Swagger Wagon"? A few of the most memorable online-only ads include Google's "How It Feels [through Glass]," Microsoft's "Child of the 90s," Kmart's "Ship My Pants," and Dove's "Real Beauty." Run a quick search on YouTube of those titles, and you will find them. Content creation is shifting from traditional entertainment companies to big tech and just about anyone with a camera. Consumer-product companies may soon be in a conundrum of where to advertise. Will they reinvent the soap-opera concept? The Ed Artz speech I mentioned was given at an annual meeting of the American Association of Advertising Agencies, where he recognized that "if we don't influence [changing technologies] and if we don't harness them—loyalty to our brands could suffer in the long term." He predicted that if advertising was no longer needed to pay most of the cost of home entertainment, then advertisers will have a hard time achieving the results they need. He was right. And the question for companies now becomes, where do they fit in the content matrix?

Big tech companies have not just invested in content; they have also invested in the future distribution channels—new top-level domains. Google is launching not just dot-YouTube—which can be segmented into subchannels like tennis.youtube or travel.youtube—but also the top-level domain dot-channel. So Bethany Mota may want Bethany.channel to build out her future enterprises, tapping into the power of Google's products and services as a package deal.

With half the world's top brands launching their own generic top-level domains or channels of the Internet, the concept of building out content in these new spaces will shift how we consume our entertainment and how consumer-goods companies reach their target audiences. The idea of the soap opera with its sponsors may emerge in new segmented spaces on brand channels of the Internet. Interestingly, Procter & Gamble did not apply for any top-level domains, despite its former CEO's advice to the ad industry to recognize, influence, and participate in changing technology. Maybe next round.

## Digital in the Boardroom

As T-Mobile's CEO Legere is also predicting, content will be delivered via the Internet in the future. It's interesting to note that this company did not apply for top-level domains either (neither did Verizon). This means megamergers in the future for cable and telecommunications, because one will become obsolete. We already see these types of mergers occurring with AT&T's purchase of DirecTV. This creates an interesting convergence of technology, distribution, and the entertainment and content businesses. YouTube is working deals with DreamWorks Animation and Awesomeness TV to produce original series with YouTube stars. Likewise, companies like Snapchat and Periscope have put consumers in the producer's seat, showing that viral video created by anyone can be just as entertaining as content created by big producers with mega budgets.

In researching patents being filed by all of these companies, we can see trends forming as traditional telecom companies invest in patented technology to deliver faster and better content via devices, tracking consumers across device platforms to deliver the best possible content service. For example, companies like Verizon are boosting their ad technology. In 2015, we saw the emergence of more and more patents related to advertising, whether it's ad blocking or more effective ad delivery.

According to *Advertising Age*, the premier ad-industry publication, the number of people actively blocking ads in the United States rose to forty-five million, up 48 percent from the previous year. Companies like Hulu and Facebook are actually looking at how users can select ads they want to see, giving consumers ultimate control over their entertainment experience. They will still be exposed to ads, but of their own choosing. YouTube is reprogramming itself to respond to these changes. YouTube is engineering its app to help people more quickly get the videos they want and is becoming the central source of entertainment for the next generation. Combined with Google's semantic intelligence, the company's ability to deliver what individuals want is a big signal to this paradigm shift that we have been talking about here. All of these signals help us understand the importance of content: content designed to connect with consumers, content created by consumers and your business, and the changing outlets and channels where that content is consumed.

## Jennifer Wolfe

In just the second quarter of 2015 alone, we could find patent activity by Adobe, Amazon, AOL, Apple, Google, eBay, Facebook, Hulu, Turner Broadcasting, Verizon, and Yahoo! related to controlling ad pricing, user interaction with ads, geolocation, or cross-browser tracking (meaning as you move from Internet explorer to chrome), delivery of ads, and measuring actual consumer awareness of ads.

With users in greater control than ever, if you want to reach a target consumer or a new consumer, you have to create content of interest in microsite bites. Whether it becomes product placement or sponsored programs like the original soap opera, there are platforms available that don't cost anything if you can generate viral interest. I've noted that YouTube is the second-largest search engine in the world. I watch my thirteen-year-old and his friends discuss YouTube as though it's the primary channel of entertainment. Brands know this, and if they can get kids or other targeted demographics to watch them on YouTube and then link them into their spaces, they can hook consumers on more content and succeed that way. This is the future of advertising and marketing. It's no longer linear but programmatically based on pulling in consumers with great content delivered through a variety of digital media and mathematically determined.

When we look at our digital maps, we can recognize that content can be delivered in all of the digital channels (online in microsites, apps and mobile, social media—anywhere in the vast Internet space that content can be streamed). No one place mutually excludes another. But it's now about creating a holistic experience. Whom does your company target? How will they access content about your brand? An ad interruption is not likely going to work in the future; rather, engaging content across the digital ecosphere will create loyal brand followers.

"Customers are all looking for relevant communication that relates directly to their needs—it doesn't matter if they're searching for a product or service... Understanding how, why, and when your customers engage with certain channels will lead to a better customer experience and ultimately more sales," says a trend analysis in *Marketing Land Buying Behavior*, a leading online publication on consumer behavior.

In the ad business, not only are companies moving toward programmatic ad buying, where computers electronically place the ads, but also, they must actually get better creatively. Consumers are seeking out the programs they want; advertisers will no longer place images in content delivered by distributors. The lines are no longer clear. Agencies and ad-tech companies have emerged to meet this need, helping companies solve this increasingly changing and challenging marketplace. Without a doubt, the changes are here and will continue. Let's look at a few other signals of this change in content.

## HOW GOOGLE, AMAZON, ROKU, AND APPLE TV WILL CHANGE EVERYTHING ABOUT CONTENT

One of the single greatest boosts for the value of the content delivered via the Internet is Google's Chromecast, particularly for companies already in the content-distribution business. At thirty-five dollars, delivered in two days free from Amazon Prime, it transforms your tablet, phone, or computer into a remote control to surf the Internet on almost any flat-screen in your house for Chromecast-enabled content. While the trend toward consumption of content via the Internet is nothing new, and other devices like Apple TV and Roku provide Internet-based TV access, Chromecast's cost-effectiveness and ease of use of means the less tech savvy can sit on their couches and search the Internet. This simple device could push the tipping point on Internet consumption of content.

Apple's CEO Tim Cook fired back at the *Wall Street Journal* when he was questioned if Apple TV had not transformed TV in the way it had expected to:

> When you really look at the TV experience today, the TV makes the decision about what time to watch it. Or we have to decide whether to record it in advance. If I come to work the next day and hear about something that happened last night that I didn't see, if I haven't recorded it, maybe I can find it somewhere on the web, maybe I can't. We've developed a whole infrastructure to try to fix this broken process.

On the flip side, the continuing consolidation of the cable industry with Comcast's bid to acquire Time Warner Cable means there will be fewer choices in cable providers and more choices online. For the millions of Americans who still rely upon cable as the only source for content on their flat-screens, the consolidation and potential change in offerings and pricing could be enough to push them over the technology edge.

Interestingly, Comcast applied for several top-level domains, including dot-comcast and dot-xfinity, potentially forecasting the future shift to online distribution and arming itself with the technology it will need. Time Warner Cable, long recognized as behind the technology curve with its devices, did not apply for any top-level domains. Dish Network applied for several, including dot-blockbuster, dot-data, dot-direct, dot-dish, dot-dot, dot-dtv, dot-latino, dot-locker, dot-mobile, dot-movie, dot-ollo, dot-ott, and dot-phone. Other big cable providers include Rogers, with dot-charter, dot-fido, and dot-rogers; Echostar with dot-dvr, dot-hughes, dot-sling, and dot-stream; along with Frontier Communications (with dot-frontier and dot-ftr) and Now TV (dot-nowtv).

As the cable industry consolidates in harvest mode, the industry leaders have applied for new top-level domains, preparing for the next generation of surfing channels online. Of course, these leaders are also providing access to the Internet, so they are already in place for consumer-behavior shifts ahead.

Additionally, fiber-optic cable networks like Google Fiber, Verizon, AT&T, and others are delivering services to the home at more competitive rates, making fiber speed accessible to consumers. In the past, consumers were not willing to shell out more money for higher-speed access when it didn't make that big of a difference to them. But if they shift spending from direct cable subscriptions to fiber access, using their Google Chromecasts to turn every device into remote controls, the shift away from cable and into the digital world becomes within reach for average consumers.

In the Internet space, many traditional networks and content distributors applied for new top-level domains, including ABC, Fox, Bloomberg, CBS, Comcast, HBO, Showtime, The Weather Channel, Netflix, XBOX, PlayStation, and others. Alongside traditional content distributors, Google submitted 101 applications and Amazon, 76. The key benefit for these companies is that by owning their own top-level domains, they actually own channels of the Internet. So, if you go to guide.weather, you may be able to surf everything The Weather Channel has to offer. Likewise, Google's dot-channel could become just that. For brands, their top-level domains are completely closed and owned by them, so they can create the best possible digital experiences and track the all-important data across their own digital channels.

Other top-level domain owners who could build out channels of content include the MLB, NFL, and NBA. In the future of the digital world, consumers can access everything they want from their couches, with tablets or phones as the remotes. The top-level domains unchain these companies from the online home-page concept to create the ability to provide directories of content and unique, memorable landing pages or experiences to invite consumers into their digital worlds in new and interesting ways.

There is no question that the changing expectations of consumers to a programmatic, content-driven approach from a linear approach and the changing face of the Internet will impact how your company builds, creates, and curates content in your digital world. But what else may influence this component of the digital transformation?

Interestingly, as consumers consider cutting the cable cord and look to save money by consolidating, there is a return in some ways to an old-school bundling. Sling, for example, offers a mix of cable networks for twenty dollars a month that include a few basics like ESPN, AMC, and CNN. The Internet will supplement those core basic channels so that consumers can access whatever they want either for a fee or with program-based advertising. HBO, back in 2014, began exploring how to stream its services, recognizing that in the future, this is how people will consume their subscription-based content.

Regardless of what industry you are in, you need content. And it needs to be more robust and engaging and to change frequently. There are many forms of content that all companies will need to create. Content in the digital world can come in many forms:

* Articles
* Videos (shorts for Vine and Twitter, or longer-form videos, or episodes and series like traditional television shows to engage and hook users)

* Photographs
* Podcasts
* Infographics
* Product releases
* Demos
* Presentations
* Original music (think Starbucks)
* Original programs (like *House of Cards*)

As companies large and small look to their leadership to show them the future and look to their boards to protect their long-term interests, understanding these signals of change to predict the future will bring digital front and center in the boardroom.

When we talk about predicting the future and preparing your company for that future, the status-quo mentality often creeps in. Here are just a couple more reminders of how easily the status quo will be fought for:

* "The cinema is little more than a fad. It's canned drama. What audiences really want to see is flesh and blood on the stage." (Charlie Chaplin, 1916)
* "The wireless music box has no imaginable commercial value. Who would pay for a message sent to no one in particular?" (David Sarnoff, 1921)

They were wrong. But what's common to them? They were all fearful of their industries changing and disrupting what was comfortable, known, and secure. As you listen to senior executives in your company talk about digital and particularly how content and advertising will change, look for signs of the status-quo mentality.

Throughout this book, I've taken you through components of the digital map, an exercise that can help your company identify problems and opportunities in architecting a better digital world and leveraging content across all facets of the digital space. But now it's time to look at how we design that digital world to understand trends and drive behavior. In the next chapter, I'll focus on optimizing the digital world to build digital intelligence.

## KEY TAKEAWAYS FROM CHAPTER 7

* In the future, content will be delivered almost exclusively by the Internet.
* The ad industry is in a state of flux as the lines blur between best practices: some companies create content and then sell advertising around it, and some now simply create their own content that sells their products, distributing it via digital channels.
* All companies will increasingly need compelling content that's not just a one-way ad but a two-way relationship, deeply engaging an audience across its digital world. Content, regardless of how it is distributed and whether you produce it for yourself or sell ads to support it, will always be king.
* Where will your company fit into the content matrix?

*Chapter 8*

• • •

# BIG DATA OPTIMIZED IS DIGITAL INTELLIGENCE

For the last two decades, since dot-com became a thing and the concept of digital was formed, marketers have focused on SEO and e-commerce with traffic, impressions, click-throughs, conversions, and sales being the primary data metrics. This is because driving traffic to a website was almost the only digital goal toward generating revenue (whether by ads, click-through revenue, or e-commerce and actually selling something). But today, the digital world is a lot more complex, and the digital world produces a lot of data. *Big data* has been a buzz phrase in recent years as marketers struggle to capture it, analyze it, and do something intelligent with it.

In the future, SEO will be only one piece of the optimization puzzle. Big data from all sources in the digital world will need to be optimized to synthesize it into something that can be used and digested. Digital optimization will yield Digital Intelligence—data gathered in a strategic methodology from multiple sources, aggregated and analyzed into meaningful information to predict future trends, opportunities, and threats to an organization.

It's important to recognize that you can optimize your digital world, but you also need to gather data from the external world to ensure you truly have digital intelligence. Combining these two sources of data can yield Digital Intelligence.

Digital Intelligence is the result of companies optimizing their digital experiences so they can leverage the many sources of data and optimize how consumers use their digital worlds. Many books exist about analyzing data, but I want to focus here on sources of data—some which you may not have considered—and introduce the concept of optimizing your digital world to collect and interpret data that provides strategic insights you can use.

Digital data comes from many sources, some of which may seem obvious and some of which may not:

**E-commerce.** For companies generating revenue from online sales, e-commerce is a big piece of data to analyze. Whether you sell a subscription to content or software, sell software as a service, or still sell actual physical products that get delivered, e-commerce data tells you who buys what—when, where, and, in many cases, what prompted them to make the purchase. We can even track what they held in their cart or searched for but didn't yet buy. Algorithms by companies like Amazon have grown better and better at making predictions on buying behavior. For example, we can track in their patent activity that they are discovering new ways to share data among electronic devices and even control power consumption based on the gaze of a user or to generate ads and personalized content based on user activity.

But this data cannot be viewed in isolation, because many people arrive at a purchase point from multiple sources, and understanding all of those sources and pieces is important to seeing the bigger picture. You can gather data internally from your systems and externally from other companies that collect it.

**Social.** The revenue model for social-media companies is predicated on being able to generate meaningful data and help companies sell products and services to targeted people based upon it. Twitter and Facebook can, to the extent statistically accurate, predict how a population of people is thinking, feeling, and interacting with one another. They can't predict what's happening with people who aren't on their network, which becomes a driving force for growth.

Other social networks track data, and when it has value to other companies, can monetize it. Within your own social spaces, you can see how your brand, company, or executives are mentioned and weight that according to the types of people making those comments to discern what people like or don't like about your company, a campaign, or product at any given time.

Careful planning of how you and others talk about traditional campaigns in digital spheres can be very valuable. Likewise, monitoring feedback in the digital world provides you with insight. Such feedback will occur on everything from photos and posts to videos across all platforms, all of which can be measured and tracked.

A word of caution, however—what data you can access changes. For example, Facebook, in the fall of 2015, changed its data policy. What was once available to partners and other apps was taken away in favor of providing its customers more privacy. This impacted companies like Tinder, Redpoint Ventures, YesGraph, and others that had relied on those data sources to fuel their own apps. Accordingly, building your data structure or core business around data that you get freely may not be the best idea, because the next day, it might be gone, or you may have to pay a lot more for it, which can disrupt your business model.

Likewise, Google used to provide certain analytics for free but then took that away, leaving companies scrambling to get data points about traffic patterns. Companies may give data away at the beginning, but once a scale and mass is reached that can't be rolled back, they will likely charge for access.

Data in these spaces can be internally driven by your own social-media feedback loop—discerning what has meaning and what doesn't—and externally driven with data purchased from social-media providers (whether outright or bundled in other services).

**Mobile and geolocation tracking.** In recent years, companies like Apple, Google, Facebook, Amazon, Verizon, AT&T, and many others have been filing patents related to geolocation-tracking technology. Mobile platforms have become a beacon for knowing where a user is at any given point in time and, based upon the user's history and location, providing recommendations about what he or she might want to eat or buy. The category of patents related to user recommendations is heavily populated by technology and media companies alike, all trying to predict what consumers want and need and how to motivate them to buy or consume products and services.

The data sets on where people are and what they are doing has tremendous value when it comes to what works in online marketing and what consumers want and need. Likewise, where someone is can predict what he or she buys if the dots are connected. The Weather Channel might be able to predict that more umbrellas will be sold on a rainy day. Connect the weather patterns around a person carrying a device, and you can prompt him or her to pick up an umbrella alongside his or her Starbucks that morning. Coupons and recipes delivered to the consumer while he or she is shopping for groceries? This is made possible with geolocation tracking. This technology can be found in patents by companies like Adobe, eBay, Yahoo!, and Google.

**The Internet of things**. All of the things we talked about in chapter 6 will start to produce data. The companies that own the devices and the software will have it, and other companies may have access to it through various licensing or ad models. Imagine when you can know what your consumers eat for breakfast, what time they wake up, and what's in their refrigerators as they drive home, right by your wine shop—care to recommend something for dinner? This is the type of big data that can be captured across segments of security, health, energy usage, retail shopping, travel and logistics, and more.

**Adwords**. Adwords have been a staple of Google's success, a monetized way of promoting products and services based upon keywords. This, naturally, provides immediate data points of what is working and what isn't. By understanding which Google ads work, companies can target campaigns and strategies. Many companies will refer to not just ads but any kind of messaging as A-B testing, which is how they systematically compare ads or messages to see which works better, refining messages to create the desired result in the right places.

**Click-throughs, views, and impressions.** The other big metric that gets tracked is traditional—the number of views of any given piece of content. By tracking how many people view something, one can infer some level of popularity and response. Click-throughs tell you how many people clicked on a sponsored link to get to your content, and impressions can tell you how many people saw the ad. And, of course, conversion tells you what converts to your goal, whether it's to buy something, sign up for something, or whatever it might be that converts the person from just looking at you online to doing something with you.

**Traffic**. Traffic patterns are also important. Across your digital properties, you can track where people are coming from, the peak times of day for activity in your digital world, and assimilate that with what else is happening.

This is where clearly tying everything that's happening in your digital world is important. Tools like heat maps are also used to determine what areas of a digital property get the most attention and what needs to be reworked.

**Online behavior.** Cookies help track IP addresses (where a user is when he or she accesses the Internet), so you know when someone from a specific IP address is returning to your site. Of course, this can be problematic when numerous people use the same IP address. This is why I might get prompts based upon something my husband or son did on my computer. Many companies are trying to overcome this limitation of cookies by developing cross-device tracking technology. This is why so many companies are trying to develop technology to identify a specific user across devices and IP addresses.

Cookies, however, have become more controversial than ever. For example, in 2012, the European Union began to require organizations to secure permission before installing any cookies. Privacy concerns have become a larger issue, so CMOs must reevaluate their strategies. And understanding cross-device or cross-IP tracking is also becoming increasingly important. The patent office is filled with applications that show that companies are trying to figure this one out—and many already have.

All of us can actually turn off cookies on each device, though our favorite websites will not remember us when we return, and we'll have to reenter our usernames and passwords each time. Additionally, cookies could be enabled at the top level in the future, which could produce interesting new results for companies with Dot Brand top-level domains.

**Patents.** A piece of data that is incredibly valuable to every company but only the highly tech savvy have used, and only minimally, is the tracking of competitors' patent filings alongside those of other big technology drivers like Google, Amazon, Facebook, and Microsoft. I've been making note throughout the book of patents that I use to predict trends. Evaluating patent filings in your industry and tangential industries can help you predict important trends and is an essential piece of data in a digital age. This is largely externally driven data.

**Digital changes.** Another big piece of data is in tracking and monitoring the use of keywords about your company and your brand as they show up in new digital properties. Through web-monitoring services, you can track

## Digital in the Boardroom

when your competitors are adding new digital properties or when something with bad intentions starts copying or using your name, content, or information. Watching for these is often relegated to lawyers, but any such activity is a critical piece of information to understand if it's happening anywhere in the digital ecosystem (especially social spaces).

**Consumer behavior across digital.** Your digital properties are gathering all of these data sets into a big pot of consumer behavior: where do people search, what prompts them to buy, what do they buy, and where is it sent? What prompts them to return to a digital property, and how frequently do they return? What are the hot spots on your digital properties where consumers spend most of their time?

**Properties that do not exist.** Companies with their own top-level domains will be able to track any domain names Internet users type into the browser that don't exist. This can give insight into landing pages or spaces that consumers may want from your company that you currently don't offer.

**Technology mapping.** Another source of external data is to track how mergers and acquisitions consolidate technology, supply chains, or data sets. This requires mapping out technology groups and access to supply chains or data to understand how all of that activity consolidates choices or allows for greater economies of scale.

**The future.** There will be new platforms, new sources for data, and new ways to gather data. This will constantly change and needs constant attention.

According to a report by IBM, "The biggest challenge isn't the amount of data that's available, but interpreting the data and making business decisions based upon insights it provides. Data analytics will allow us to test our assumptions." We gather lots of data, but we need to put data sets together in ways that may not have made sense in the past. When we look at the whole, we may be able to better predict the trends that are so critical to business success. Hal Varian, chief economist at Google, says, "I keep saying that the sexy job in the next ten years will be statisticians, and I'm not kidding." Ginni Rometty, CEO of IBM, adds, "Big data will spell the death of customer segmentation and force the marketer to understand each customer as an individual within eighteen months or risk being left in the dust."

The expansion of data from internal and external sources is overwhelming. There are many methodologies for crunching all of those numbers and finding patterns or trends that matter. All of this data means we can pull together how and why people behave the way they do. But we can also harness the data not just for more profits but for social good. How do we tie it together into Digital Intelligence?

There are companies providing expertise in data analytics, such as SAS, IBM, Omniture, and many others. *Forbes* magazine cited InsightSquared, Paxata, and Trifacta as a few of the top-rated data companies to work for in 2015. The key is to use these resources to help you navigate this vast space and also to design your digital world so you can optimize all those data points.

An emerging best practice is to have a data architect design your company's digital world much like an architect would design a neighborhood. I refer to this has optimizing your Digital Map (see Figure 8.1). Of course, there is software to help crunch numbers and find meaning in the chaos, but an architect designs the digital map for your company. The technology will only continue to improve the tools to analyze and pull all your data together.

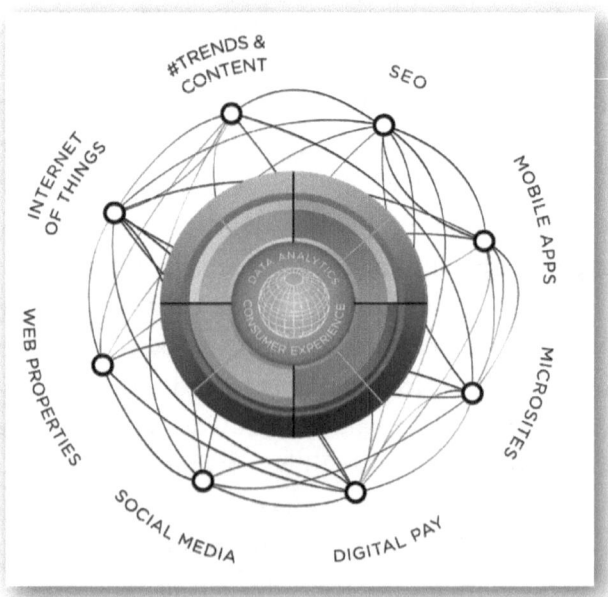

Fig. 8.1. Digital map, optimized

But, in the boardroom, what do you really need to know? Throughout this book, I've talked about looking for signals of change—pushing against assumptions and not believing that things won't change. As you consider your digital neighborhood, think about how you want consumers to navigate online from social to the Internet of things or mobile devices. Connect all of the components in your design to optimize the experience and optimize your ability to track and leverage data.

## EXTERNAL DATA SIGNALS IN THE BOARDROOM

I'd like to focus on two big drivers of change in data that, when optimized and incorporated into a digital data strategy, could create a plan and an architecture for your digital universe in a new way. Most companies largely overlook these because both have been relegated to lawyers who focus more on risk management than identifying opportunities. I've already spoken about them separately, but I want to bring them together here: **top-level domains** (i.e., the future of the Internet experience) and **patents** (i.e., where digital is investing). Looking at these drivers together can help digital marketers forecast changes that impact your company. Consider how looking at these new channels of the Internet and new patents together can help you identify trends. These are two external forces at work.

You might not think that generic top-level domains and patents have much in common. But if you compare the new top-level domains that big companies plan to operate to their recent patent filings, you might spot some trends.

Take Comcast, for example. As I've mentioned, Comcast applied for dot-comcast and dot-xfinity. Comcast has filed 65 percent of its 241-strong patent portfolio *in the last three years* and recently filed patent applications for inventions like:

* "a recommendation system"
* "playlists within a network"
* "predictive content caching"
* "crowdsourcing supplemental content"

While these phrases are merely from titles of complex patent applications, it's enough data to start to show a pattern of where the company might be headed. Comcast knows cable is in decline. So, while it harvests a business model in its final phases, it's preparing for what comes next. It's buying generic top-level domains that could be used as distribution channels. It's investing in patentable technology to help consumers use that generic-top-level-domain platform, or other technology for that matter, when consumers shift from cable-based entertainment to Internet-based entertainment.

Time Warner Cable, on the other hand, did not apply for any generic top-level domains. It has a portfolio of 281 patents, with 60 percent filed in the last three years, but they're heavily focused on pictorial communication or television rather than digital data processing or transmission of digital information. Is it that surprising that Time Warner needs an exit strategy?

But Google, which applied for just over a hundred new generic top-level domains, and Amazon, with seventy-six, are expanding their digital-patent portfolios. Google has 10,625 patents, with nearly half of them issued in the last three years. Amazon has 2,006 issued patents, and 77 percent were issued in the last three years. Some recent Google filings name:

* "customizable media channels"
* "interfaces to allow video ad serving into a mobile phone application video stream"
* "recommending media programs based on media program popularity"
* "social aspects of media guides"
* "self-service channel marketplace"
* "presenting mobile content based on programming content"

And some recent Amazon filings propose:

* "providing gift clustering to assist a user in ordering multiple items for a recipient"
* "securing content using a wireless authentication factor"
* "surface-based location determination"
* "speech-based shopping"

### Digital in the Boardroom

These are only a few among many across a wide range of their services, from logistics to the consumer digital experience.

## WHAT PATENTS TELL US

In the United States, we live in a first-to-file system. The first company to file for a patent typically acquires it. This means that big companies file for patents as soon as they think they have something valuable. Once the patent is published, it's publicly available, and you can track trends about who is filing for what and review basic technology areas to plot onto predictive graphs. In the boardroom, this becomes essential data to help you predict the future and identify some of your company's areas of weakness.

For example, recent patent filings show that Yahoo! is building a personal video inbox and that Hulu and AOL are beefing up their patent portfolios. Google and Disney are both preparing for phones and tablets to be used as remote controls.

Monitoring what patents are being filed, particularly in a rapidly changing digital environment, can help you see where companies are headed, what new services they might soon try to sell, or how they may try to push consumer behavior. It can also signal when traditional media, consumer goods, or retail companies are gearing up for a digital play. While some of what we see in them may simply be logical next steps, patent filings show specifics and can give you a competitive edge if you pay attention to the signs.

And don't forget about design patents. Design patents can sometimes predict future trends that are not always numbers-based. The famous Samsung-Apple patent battle, which is still on appeal after years in court, was largely over design. The patent at issue was about the curved corners of the icons on the phone. Even Batman is patented by his owner, DC Comics, to ensure that no other superhero can knock off his iconic style.

Fig. 8.2. Batman patent drawing

Surprisingly, powerhouse companies like Google have only recently started using patents. The Google patent department didn't really even exist before 2012. In an *IAM* article, Allen Lo, head of the Google Patent Group, says, "Part of what we've been doing is not just leveraging commercially available tools and becoming knowledgeable…but also leveraging resources…Whether it's from engineering, from our economists, or other parts of the company, we ask, 'How do we get smarter about understanding patents…Whether it be trends or greater insights—to understand our portfolio, understand the portfolio of others, understand how things are being transacted. We need to develop that expertise and really develop and institutionalize it.'"

These vast sources of data, and the need to design your digital world to optimize it, are why your company also needs a chief digital officer.

In the 1980s, companies did not have chief information officers or chief technical officers—there was no need. Up until now, it has worked to embed digital functions within marketing or IT. But that is changing. Some companies refer to this as omnichannel, but it really is about connecting all of the digital dots. A company's cybersecurity plan must integrate with the creation of a digital experience for the customer and how you as a company use all of the data you can track as a result. It's a big undertaking that can sometimes put the CIO and the CMO at odds and is often untapped because of a status-quo mentality or competing interests somewhere.

Digital requires something from all of these roles, and that means you may need a senior executive focused on crossing over these divides and finding the best path forward for your company. In the boardroom, you need to be armed with data to question senior leadership, challenge it, and push it to ensure that you fulfill your collective oversight role. As a director, you can access important external data points and ensure your senior executive team is equipped to lead through these changing digital times.

## WHY COMPANIES NEED CHIEF DIGITAL OFFICERS

Companies are digitally innovating faster than ever, as digital assets are often at the center of today's marketing and social-media initiatives. The list is long, but some of the significant initiatives include user interfaces, apps, social-networking functions, personalization options on web pages, subscriber perks, and new products and services related to digital assets. As this world inherently cuts across long-standing company silos, forward-looking companies are arming themselves with a new senior executive—the chief digital officer or CDO—whose purpose is to bridge the fragmented corporate environment by connecting marketing, social-media, IT, research-and-development, intellectual-property, and privacy experts and other key stakeholders to ensure digital assets are being developed and utilized strategically.

For a company that doesn't have a CDO—or if the CDO's role is undefined, underutilized, or unclear, a CMO and the marketing team have a tremendous opportunity and responsibility to help shape the role of the CDO and break down the cross-department silos that exist today so that marketing can fully leverage and integrate with all aspects of digital. In many instances, if marketing doesn't take the lead in shaping the role, then IT will, and it will be driven from an IT lens versus a marketing lens.

While there are many functions to the role of the CDO, integrating with marketing is most central to long-term success. Additionally, the role of the CDO can bolster marketing if cultivated in a way that integrates the many facets of digital strategy into the overall company marketing strategy. The CDO can help bridge the gap between technology and marketing. Without leadership from marketing in developing and empowering the role, digital in your company may never realize its full potential. Or, worse, it may spin off into its own silo and be counterproductive to traditional marketing initiatives.

A few leading companies have already announced the CDO role. Microsoft, Starbucks, the *Washington Post*, Lincoln Financial, TOMS, and even universities such as Harvard and MIT have restructured with CDOs. These smart, forward-looking organizations understand the evolving role of digital in business today and recognize that having digital fragmented across groups was not effectively tapping into the power of digital strategy and assets. For example, most CDOs tackle building social-media engagement platforms and then connect those platforms with e-commerce, Wi-Fi strategies (for brick-and-mortar outlets), mobile applications, and other functions as a starting point to building return on investment for digital efforts.

Additionally, bridging offline and online experiences is essential as a first step—this inherently requires a connection to and understanding of marketing. Recent leading industry reports show that companies now spend more on social media, apps, and mobile messaging than on traditional media. For most companies, this is a departure from past days of marketing, covering everything from market and consumer research to television, product placement, couponing, promotions, print, sponsorship, radio, and other traditional advertising and marketing efforts. Social-media departments have popped up across companies or are outsourced to specialty agencies focused on Facebook, Twitter, Pinterest, web design, apps, and mobile messaging, to name just a few. With these activities often parsed out to separate brand managers, few organizations have yet tied them all under one strategic digital roof where economies of scale and better implementation could prevail.

In the last twenty years, we have evolved from the information age into a digital age, requiring CMOs to learn a whole new language, not to mention how these days of big data are changing every aspect of how organizations are run. Now savvy marketers recognize the valuable data and intelligence driven from digital-related marketing efforts. As the very fabric of our lives is in the digital space—from Facebook and Twitter to Pandora, Groupon, and eBay—it's now generally accepted that most consumers are spending more time online or in mobile messaging than in any other media. Every piece of data that we need to respond to market demands comes from a digital world. In other words, the reach of digital is too broad to be housed in any existing department and warrants its own leader. In the boardroom, now is the time to get engaged in defining that role.

## THE ROLE OF THE CDO

The role of the CDO is to provide strategic direction on how the company leverages its digital assets and reputation in a digital world. A CDO works in collaboration with the CMO, who is largely responsible for all marketing efforts in more traditional distribution methods and ensures that the digital strategy is in sync with those. The CDO taps into data and research that may be valuable for innovation or other activities throughout the company and centralizes it into knowledge-sharing tools. Since this is the most valuable information the company is gathering (i.e., the data collected through digital tracking), it should be shared from top to bottom. If it remains fragmented, then the company is likely wasting money reworking the same tasks in different divisions and with varying data sets without a unifying, cohesive strategy. If marketing helps shape the role, then it ensures the ability to capture this knowledge and redirect it into its traditional marketing strategy.

In addition to working with the CMO, the CDO crosses over divides to work with the CIO, CLO, and corporate communications to ensure that the reputation of the company is monitored and information is distributed, brands and assets are protected, privacy issues are evaluated and audited regularly, and the technical infrastructure of its digital assets are properly developed in sync with legacy company technology. All of these issues have exploded in a complex technical and litigious global marketplace requiring careful management of new exposure to liability and technical infrastructure. Communication across these stakeholder groups is critical, but strategic alignment is the key to success.

A CDO also helps a company integrate e-commerce into a cohesive strategy to utilize data to drive other marketing initiatives. As more marketers become content creators versus just marketers or advertisers, the need for data about consumer choice is essential to drive the creation of new entertainment created by marketers for consumers.

Starbucks, for example, launched its Starbucks Digital Network to not only provide Wi-Fi to customers but also to stream fresh, local, and valuable content as a content curator, enhancing the overall consumer experience. Starbucks's CDO has gone a step further into driving social innovation through job initiatives and other social movements via digital platforms as part of its focus.

## THE RETURN ON INVESTMENT OF THE CDO

At its core, return on investment can be calculated with data points by determining the profit and loss of digital initiatives. Marketing should be involved in this modeling to ensure it does not lose its allocation of the credit for company revenues. In addition to the traditional profit-and-loss statement, a few other advantages for the company include eliminating the rework and unfocused work associated with fragmentation of digital initiatives across departments. The use of data analytics could be widely distributed across departments to improve overall company performance.

For example, the same data that helps detect counterfeiting or brand infringement can also be used to help corporate communications stop rumors or do reputation management, or to redirect important data points to research and development as key consumer insights for potential new products, all without investing in costly outside studies. Strategy can be driven from a top level, ensuring that messaging is always on track.

A CDO also works to eliminate digital blunders with more focused strategy and implementation. How many companies and CEOs have gotten in trouble because of tweets, posts on Facebook, or texts gone awry?

The role of the CDO is emerging and will become more important as the pace at which we live our lives in the digital world increases. Forward-thinking companies are beginning to look at this as an important next step in the evolution of the corporate structure. Savvy marketing executives can lead the changing landscape by shaping the role of the CDO to strategically integrate and align with marketing initiatives.

Fig. 8.3. Digital leadership

## Digital in the Boardroom

Your CDO will need to audit your existing digital experience and cybersecurity practices and evaluate how you can create a better digital experience. Consider the digital mapping exercise I've referenced throughout this book. This is about evaluating each component of the digital experience and understanding how consumers navigate among the sectors of the map: What's working? What isn't? How can you drive consumer behavior and track that data? How can you give consumers choices and see how they respond? How can you leverage the fact that consumers go from social to mobile, into your microsites, and then back out to your home page? How can you track what they search for when they get to you? How can you track when they go somewhere else, and why? How can you make a digital experience that crosses over from any real-life experience consumers have with you so great that they will want it over and over, or so convenient or cheap they will choose you over competitors?

It's hard to expect the CIO to address these questions. In a 2014 *Wall Street Journal* study, CIOs indicated that their biggest priority and concern was business intelligence and analytics. Can they really tackle that plus infrastructure, cloud, mobile, and cybersecurity?

Consider these steps in the optimization process:

1. **Create your digital map.** To start the optimization process, you must understand where you fit in your consumer's digital world. The key is to ask questions of your team about all facets of digital and gather this data on a regular basis to optimize how consumers navigate from one space to the next so that you truly design and architect your digital world to gather the data you want and provide the experience consumers want.

2. **Unchain your home page.** The home page is a massive, sprawling space trying to do too many things. The search engines have to crawl a lot of content to find anything related to what the searcher is seeking. By building out smaller, niched spaces, you can not only focus on what the consumer really wants in that space, but you can also make it easier for search engines to identify and crawl your sites—particularly in an age of quality over quantity of keywords, backlinks, and so

on. The more qualitatively focused your digital address is, the higher it will rise in organic search.
3. **Integrate your social and mobile strategies.** Connect the credibility associated with your brand into these already-trusted spaces. Understanding the intersection of how consumers interact with you from one platform to the next can provide key data sets.
4. **Integrate with cybersecurity.** Connect everything your company does with its cybersecurity strategy and ensure that all points are aligned. The cybersecurity dashboard suggested in chapter 3 is a great starting point, but it needs to be maintained and cross-checked with the digital strategy and be added to critical data points to drive future decisions.
5. **Focus on the user experience.** Build better digital experiences across platforms. The easier you make it for consumers, the more the algorithms will recognize you for quality and authenticity. What will be important, today and moving forward, is embracing the mix, getting the mix right, and repeating that success using these newer tactics.

These are the questions your CDO should be asking about user experience:

* Who are the members of your audience?
* Why do they come into your digital world?
* How do they come into your digital world?
* What do they do while they are there?
* Are they frustrated, or can they find what they need? How do you know?
* Are they easily swayed to a competitor? Why?
* What problem are you solving? Can you do that across platforms and media?
* What do you want consumers to do when they come into your digital world?
* What type of experience do they have?
* Are you active enough and tracking data to know what and how they are responding?

* How does the real-world or offline experience connect them, in and out of the digital experience?
* How can they get to you across their digital worlds (e.g., social and mobile)?

Developing a strategic plan that answers all of the above questions is the first step to optimizing your company's digital world. With so many changes coming in digital transformation, companies need a leader who reports to the CEO and the board about what each firm is doing to manage its data, optimize its digital world, and be prepared to compete in a digitally connected world.

## DON'T FORGET TO BREATHE

One final bit of commentary. As I continue to work with companies across the globe on their strategies for the future of the Internet, I've found a few commonalities, regardless of industry. Everyone is so busy with his or her "day job" that it's hard to really get a team mobilized around new ideas. As a result, many issues are left unresolved.

Rooms are filled with executives across functions in the business. Lawyers, marketers, and technology specialists all have their own road maps and priorities and are many times still addressing legacy problems. As they face increasing pressure to decrease budgets and increase output, very few organizations are able to pause and really rethink digital.

As I pondered this problem several years ago, I reflected on a trip to South Africa for an ICANN meeting, where I extended my time to travel and spent a day on a boat watching whales and dolphins outside of Cape Town. Dolphins and whales live most of their lives in the water but, as you know, need air to breathe. Similarly, to succeed in business, we live most of our lives on the go, moving so fast just to keep up and responding rapidly to manage day-to-day activities. But how do dolphins and whales remember to come up for air? What if they get so caught up in whatever all the others are doing around them down there that they forget to come up to breathe? They'd die, right?

Today, our digital world is moving so fast, and we are so caught up in following the 24-7 alerts and messaging, responding to what's happening, that we might forget to come up for air—meaning to stop and think about the future or changes on the horizon that will alter our current environments. Coming up for air allows us to think about what's important to our customers and to the future of our businesses, particularly when tackling a paradigm shift opportunity like digital transformation.

We can't forget to breathe fresh life into our businesses and our lives because of the fast-paced world that keeps pulling us deeper and deeper into the abyss of daily digital life.

The way people on Planet Earth use the Internet is changing in a dramatic way. It's not just one thing; it's all of these things collectively that change it. Every business is impacted by it. None will be saved without considering how it connects to businesses and consumers in a digital world. Never before has the Internet transformed at this scale over such a short time. There are clear strategies that need to be nurtured by a team that recognizes the depth of the opportunity. It's not often we get advance notice of a potential paradigm shift in the most important communication tool of our time. Take time to think about how this could change everything and what you can do with your digital world when it's carefully planned. Your digital world is your digital asset. How you create it, nurture it, and cultivate it is critical to your future success.

In the boardroom, what's important to recognize is that this can no longer be just a niched area of the business focused on customer experience and engagement; it truly needs to be holistic, crossing over the many facets of the company that it impacts. For digital optimization to work, however, there must be leadership that sets a culture of digital. So many companies think they aren't digital—they are manufacturing or product driven, or whatever the line is. But every company is digital. Every company must be digital, and it's time to start optimizing that digital data and experience.

Bob Wehling, former global marketing officer of Procter & Gamble, once told me the following:

> A great brand will be consistent and dependable to its loyal consumer, always delivering or exceeding expectations. The greatest brands will always strive for the highest quality, never cutting corners, and every message in marketing and advertising will reinforce that promise. For

the consumer, a great brand is one that he or she would choose over any competitor.

While Bob retired from Procter & Gamble in 2001, long before *digital* was even a buzzword, his statement remains true. The experience is still what matters; it's just now in a digital world.

## DIGITAL OPTIMIZATION IN THE DATA REVOLUTION

The board knows that data is important but has likely left it as an "in the weeds" exercise for managers somewhere down the line of the organization. But data is becoming so powerful, and the need to optimize your digital world changing so quickly, that it's time the board starts to consider these digital issues as part of its work. There are really three pieces to consider at the board and senior-management levels:

1. Access to data analysis to understand trends, threats, and opportunities to your core business
2. Using data for checks and balances with senior management to ensure that a status-quo mentality does not undermine your business
3. Tapping into new tools to share knowledge and information easily

When I researched my first book, *Brand Rewired*, my team and I learned from interviews with key executives in Fortune 500 companies that to effectuate any kind of change about innovation, you need leadership. Jacqueline Leimer, former vice-president and associate general counsel of Kraft Foods, explains how important such leadership was at Kraft: "Irene Rosenfeld, Kraft Foods' chairman and CEO, really set the tone from the top down that innovation was important. When company leadership understand the importance of innovation from the consumer level, the entire company falls into step with that way of thinking." As the board, you can work with your CEO and senior management to ensure that your company's leadership sets a tone for the digital age and then creates the processes to drive behavior and the incentives to reward it.

Ten to fifteen years ago, the buzz was about innovation. Today, it's about digital and big data. How will your organization optimize the digital experience and not only use your data but design your digital world to get the data you want? In an October 2015 *Wall Street Journal* report on big data's promises, Jerry Wolfe, CEO of Vivanda Inc., says that big data is top down: "For all the CEOs in the room, you can't delegate this." PricewaterhouseCooper's *Annual Corporate Directors Survey* found that an increasing number of board members feel they are moderately involved in business intelligence and use of big data and how to leverage data and emerging technologies.

Digital optimization is about architecting your modern digital world in a strategic and intentional way to produce data you can use to improve your performance and deliver a better user experience. Digital Intelligence is when you combine your data with external signals to identify future trends. The two are equally important in the boardroom. You need to function at a macro level. Big data has often been mired in micro-level analysis. Your job in the boardroom and in the C-suite is to see the forest for the trees. It can no longer be one part of someone's job. It needs to be someone's full-time job to report to senior management and the board on how a holistic digital strategy will help you not just survive, but succeed.

## KEY TAKEAWAYS FROM CHAPTER 8

* The amount of internal data from your digital resources and external data to predict future trends is so vast that it can hardly be added to the already-full plate of a CMO or CIO. Consider forming the role of the chief digital officer to look at the organization's digital world holistically, bringing these important pieces together.
* The future of leveraging big data will be in optimizing the digital world so that your customers have the best possible experience, yielding you data and information that helps you continually improve performance.
* In the boardroom, gathering important data can help ensure the right checks and balances are in place to provide the necessary oversight and ability to ask critical questions of senior management.

*Chapter 9*

# DIGITAL IN THE BOARDROOM

The role of digital in the boardroom and in the C-suite has changed dramatically in the last few years. Board and executive surveys support this role becoming increasingly important. News headlines show that times have changed. We all know it. Understanding, managing, and predicting what will happen in the digital world is increasingly complex, and even if digital is your core business, like it is for so many tech start-ups, it's changing so rapidly, even the experts can hardly keep up.

So, let's recap with best practices for what boards need to know and should be doing about digital in the boardroom. And then I will close out with where we began—looking for signals of change to be prepared for the future.

## DEFINE THE ROLE OF DIGITAL IN THE BOARDROOM FOR YOUR COMPANY

Most boards focus their agendas on the stalwart functions: compensation, audit, finance, and managing risk to provide the fiduciary oversight of the CEO and senior executives that they owe to shareholders of the company. For most companies, there has never been a marketing committee; it has been left to the CEO to manage with his or her team. And some boards have started digital or incorporated cybersecurity into a committee, but most have not formally addressed these issues. According to the National Association of Corporate

Directors (NACD), 67 percent of directors surveyed want more time to focus on strategy oversight and IT issues and 65 percent want more time related to cybersecurity.

As you have read through all of the functions of digital around my Digital Map and considered how that works in your organization and where it intersects with you in the boardroom, do you have a good sense of the digital strategy in your company? Do you think these things affect your company's future? Will status-quo thinking prevent you in the boardroom from knowing about some of these emerging trends that could make or break your company? Should you oversee cybersecurity like you do audit or risk exposure? Should you oversee digital to understand digital threats to the core business model that impact shareholders? Every company has a slightly different approach to where the board crosses over its mandate as oversight into management, and I am certainly not suggesting that a board do so, as that can be detrimental to the CEO's ability to lead and to the team's ability to execute on strategies set by senior executives.

But your board should define what its role is based upon the specifics of your company, because if you haven't defined it and the digital world decides you aren't keeping up, your shareholders won't be happy. And if you fail to survive a cyberattack because you didn't have the right checks and balances in place to see the risk, shareholders won't be happy then, either. So it's time for boards to define their roles. Here are a few best practices.

**Form a digital committee.** Create a committee that meets with senior executives and ensures that there is a cybersecurity plan and a holistic digital strategy for the company. This is important oversight for senior management's development of a plan, following the plan, and having checks and balances in place. This committee should work to ensure that all facets of digital and data are being considered at a macro level and that silos or status-quo thinking have not downshifted your effects into the weeds.

This committee can ensure there is high-level thinking across the organization about digital. It can oversee these functions across key leadership roles in the company.

Reporting to the digital committee should be

## Digital in the Boardroom

a. The CMO, on marketing and how the consumer is connecting to the company in the digital world
b. The CIO or CTO, to ensure that the cybersecurity plan is in place, tested, and continually improving
c. The CLO, on how privacy, intellectual property, and Internet policy are being considered
d. The CEO, providing insights into the future strategy of the company and on signals of change that are coming
e. The CDO, to report directly on how the company is building a holistic approach to digital

The digital committee should then ensure that coordination and checks and balances exist among these groups, that their interests are aligned, and that they share resources. The digital committee should concern itself with mobile and the Internet of things, the online experience, social media, e-commerce, security, and the future of the Internet. This level of oversight is essential to ensuring that status-quo thinking does not impede the company so that it misses opportunities or, worse, suffer a catastrophic blow from changes in the marketplace.

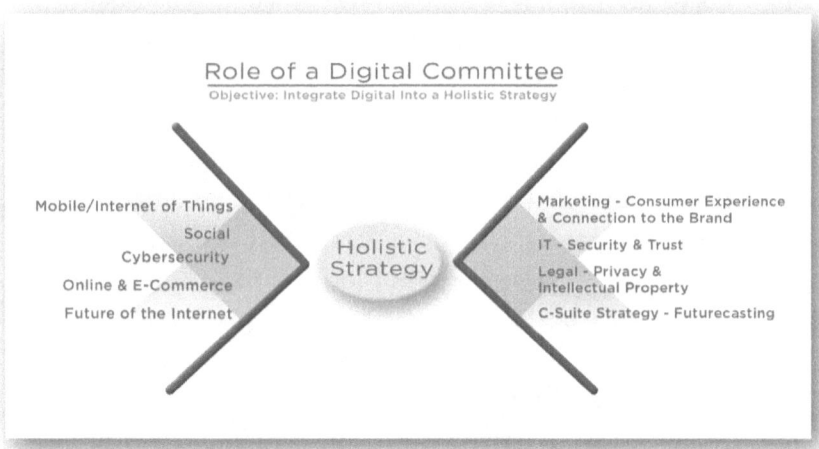

Fig. 9.1. Role of a digital committee

**Hire a chief digital officer.** I wrote at length in chapter 8 about the role of the CDO. You can encourage your CEO to have the CDO report directly to him or her so that you as the board get briefed and updated regularly. If digital is buried under marketing or IT, then your briefings may not include all of the information you need to have. Consider the role of a CDO and the benefits it could provide to your company in an age where digital is critical. Asking the CLO, CIO, or CMO to do a second full-time job might meet the political demands of the current C-suite structure but could also undermine your ability to have a leader clearly focused on one of the most important components of your business.

At the board level, you need to get a clear assessment of the digital state of your company on at least an annual basis. The CDO may have to work in tandem with the other C-suite executives, but that helps to create those checks and balances.

**Redefine or reassert the board's role.** The board is not to solve the problem or find the strategy but to ensure that someone is looking out for problems and reporting them—and that you have a strategy so you can perform your functions. Define this clearly with senior executives so that they understand the level of accountability expected and the ramifications of resulting failures.

**Plan a digital retreat.** If you have not spent a lot of time discussing digital in your board meetings, it may be time to schedule a half-day or full-day retreat to fully debrief on how your company is managing these threats and opportunities and how it approaches a holistic digital strategy. Board agendas are already packed with little time for additional information, so carving out a day to spend just on this issue may be extremely valuable in defining your role at the outset on digital and understanding the current state of digital intelligence in your organization. Schedule a retreat and consider a few sample agenda items. Be sure to bring in outside experts to educate and provide insights on some, or all, of these topics:

- Cybersecurity. Get a briefing and review of the company plan (how you are preparing, practicing, and improving on a continual basis)
- Digital threats
- Digital opportunities

- Data and how it's used across the organization
- Forecasting the future based upon the signals and data
- Audit, prepare, practice in action
- Social-media training for board members
  - Do's and don'ts
  - Privacy threats
  - Changing settings on smart devices and social media networks to protect you from yourselves

**Perform a digital audit.** Once you have defined your role and done a deep dive into understanding the threats, risk, and opportunities to your company in digital, plan for an annual digital-health check. Much like financials are audited, digital (meaning everything we just discussed, from cybersecurity to new Internet policies, new data, and how to bring it all together) should be audited to ensure your company leaders are working together and there are checks and balances in place. Think about the financial crisis that led to the need to separate accounting and audit functions and the importance of having checks and balances to ensure that one viewpoint does not dominate and expose the company to risk.

The same philosophy should apply in the digital arena. The exposure of missing something is too high to assume it's being taken care of. You need to *ensure* you audit your digital. So hire someone external to conduct an independent review. Asking your team to do it may be cost-effective, but it also comes with inherent biases that could skew the results. This is too important to the health of your organization to leave to an internal project manager. Hire an expert, audit all of the functions, and understand where there is overlap, where things are missing, and how your digital health can be improved.

A digital audit should include interviews and study of how all facets of the digital experience are being handled inside your company. The interviews should not just be of senior management, but also line managers to understand what problems they encounter, what the biggest concerns are, what threats they have encountered, and how they manage their resources and budgets. I've referred to the digital audit as Digital Mapping® to truly map the digital experience. But it can extend even beyond just the digital.

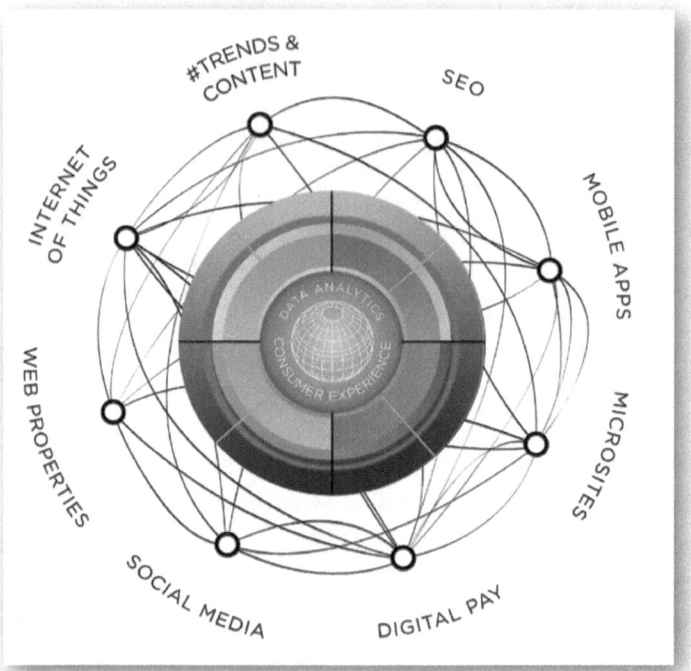

Fig. 9.2. Digital Map, optimized

**Invest in board training.** Most board members are men over the age of sixty-eight, according to PWC's annual corporate director's survey. About 49 percent of Internet users over the age of sixty-eight use social media (according to Pew Research). In the eighteen-to-forty-nine age demographic, it jumps up to 80 percent. So, it's quite possible that if you are on a board of directors of a publicly traded company, you are not addicted to Facebook or Twitter. Or you are, but personally, not professionally. You don't have to become addicted to Facebook or start a Twitter campaign to understand digital. But you do need to know how social media impacts your company and be aware of personal exposure points.

And keep in mind that this is way beyond just Facebook and Twitter. This is about deeply understanding all of the issues I discuss in this book, if you want to be able to see and spot signals of change. If you aren't familiar with any of them or many members of your board need a refresher, get some training so you can discern fact from fiction and weigh in on important issues when they're presented to you. This could be part of your digital retreat.

It can also be helpful for board members to have some one-on-one coaching to understand social media, mobile, and digital-privacy settings to ensure you know what you need to know and are prepared for what lies ahead. Most of us don't want to admit when we don't know something, so doing it in private and with a personalized approach may be more effective.

**Turn off the status-quo mentality.** Continually question if the status quo is plaguing your business. Do executives from your company say they don't like change? Are they advancing their own career agendas instead of the company's strategic goals? Will senior executives leave before the decisions they make impact you on the board? These are all very likely. It's obvious that most people don't like change, and of course they want to advance their agendas. This is human nature. It's what happens to us when we're in companies for a long time and reach a point where we want to protect ourselves or position ourselves for our next moves or exit plans. This is going to happen even in the most entrepreneurially oriented companies. But while executives leave for brighter opportunities, board members traditionally do not and will be held accountable by stakeholders.

At the board level, you need to ensure that status-quo culture is not limiting your executives' ability to see future trends and spot opportunities or prepare for serious threats. Look for clues in reports from executives. I've given examples throughout the book of paradigm shifts that weren't spotted in time.

Ask your senior executives what they read to stay on top of trends and how they push boundaries and thinking. Remember the chairman of IBM, quoted in chapter 1, who got it wrong about computers? Well, I mentioned that IBM questioned Bill Gates when he went to sell them the first computer and wanted to keep the software as a stand-alone product. IBM willingly bought the hardware and gave Bill the rights to the software. "Who would ever buy software by itself?" was likely the question.

The status quo also said to the founders of Xerox, "The world potential market for copying machines is five thousand at most." Or so they thought in 1959. IBM is obviously still around, but it's had its share of hard times and had to force innovation and dramatic shifts in its business. Imagine if it had recognized the opportunity for the computer industry in 1943, for the copy machine in 1959, or for software in the 1970s. It might be a very different company today.

**Open yourself to new opportunities.** At the board level, your job is not to innovate for the company or generate the new ideas. Your job is oversight to make sure the company is performing in the best interests of the shareholders, plain and simple. But one piece of that is to ensure that the company is thinking about the future so there is something for the shareholders in the future. When it's done well, the company might even have to split itself up. In 2015, Google divided itself into two companies to separate its core profit-making activities from its moon-rocket thinking and more research-and-development-driven activities. This is a powerful indicator of the forward-thinking concept at work.

Alphabet, Inc., the newly formed Google parent, will separate what it refers to as "far afield" from its core products. It essentially creates an innovation center for a collection of companies, perhaps the Bell Labs of the future, that has the ability to work on the future without damaging the financials of the core, for-profit business. It's really quite brilliant and will help Google maximize shareholder value out of Google's core Internet products while showing its innovative forces in big-sky thinking. It would not be surprising if Alphabet spins off a lot of other companies as its innovations become successful. Other companies could take note and build their own innovation centers and labs to create and develop free from the constraints of daily Wall Street analysts. As the board, you can help in leading this thinking and provide perspective to the CEO and executives on what could be best for the shareholders short and long term.

Boards will, undoubtedly, be under increasing pressure to be accountable for an increasingly complex state of affairs in a digital world. I'll close out this book where I began—with looking for signals of change and predicting the future. Boards, after all, are supposed to help spot trends and see the future to help CEOs navigate challenging times and make critical decisions that impact the future of organizations. To predict the future, it's important to look at internal factors (symbolized by the digital map) and external factors.

Regarding the external factors, I recommend that you

**Track and understand patent filings to know what technology is coming.** These can be big predictors of new technology or business concepts being developed and which, considered in the aggregate, can provide insights and trends. There is also software that can help you scope this research to deliver valuable results. I've shown throughout the book where patents help predict coming trends. By tracking key patent filings at a macro business level rather than a technical-claim-set level, you can get a snapshot of what big tech companies and your competitors are working on to identify trends and predict the probability that they will impact your company.

**Track historical shifts.** Track headlines in the *Wall Street Journal* and other publications about what's happening in digital, cybersecurity, and your industry. Track them over a year or two, and you'll start to pick up on the trends. Have someone on your digital team track key statistics on consumer behavior and present quarterly studies on new digital tools that people are adopting and how they are penetrating the population.

**Commit to technology mapping.** Map out mergers and deals between companies. As industries consolidate and mergers are approved, be sure to map out what technologies are being combined and what market presences may be expanded. Ask yourself how supply chains are impacted. What about access to data or ability to scale? What is one day a vendor could someday be a competitor. Big technology companies could become competitors in facets of your business—or certainly influencers. Understanding how these mergers will impact your business is an important annual mapping exercise to predict future trends.

**Know human needs.** Track which human needs are changing and evolving and what your company provides to respond to them. Consider how your company can provide for an unmet need in this changing digital environment. Think through those signals of change and ask how your company fits into them, what problems it solves, and what great experience it can create. There are many human problems; some are significant and profound, like poverty, crime, terrorism, and access to health, energy, the Internet, information, and basic human rights. Others are more trivial, though equally important in many lives, like access to social media, making life easier and more convenient, allowing more time for—well, hopefully, something important.

But we all certainly seem to want more time. Where your company fits in that spectrum is important to identifying future needs you can meet.

Predicting the future is never an exact science. No one has a crystal ball or a time machine, at least not yet. But we can look to signals and understand them both internally from data sets we have and externally with signals that can predict shifts coming. This is what digital now provides us in the boardroom.

To perform these functions, board members and senior management need to be well versed in the digital map of the company and understand where its threats and opportunities exist. In this book, I've tried to pull together the key elements of what you need to know to be ready to tackle this important issue in the boardroom. But the rest is up to you. At its most basic level, the board's role in digital really comes down to two components:

1. **Security and oversight.** Your job, first and foremost, is to make sure that the checks and balances are in place to prevent something really bad from happening.
2. **Data and the future.** You job also entails watching for data points and signals that your business model may change or whether it's directly or indirectly threatened. Or, there could just be future opportunities. Boards must ensure that their CEOs and senior management are not blinded by the status quo and set a tone and culture for the company to look for signals and keep thinking about how the continuously changing digital environment impacts the company.

Google's former chairman, Eric Schmidt, in his book *The New Digital Age*, says, "Each individual, state, and organization will have to discover its own formula, and those that can best navigate this multidimensional world will find themselves ahead of the future." The future, for most companies, will come from understanding digital in the boardroom.

## ABOUT THE AUTHOR

Jen Wolfe is the CEO of Dot Brand 360, an agency specializing in board and C-suite-level digital strategy for the next generation of the Internet and specifically how companies can use new top-level domains operating at the root zone of the Internet to bolster security, data, and user experiences across digital and technical operations. She has served as the managing partner of a prominent intellectual-property law firm—Wolfe, Sadler, Breen, Morasch and Colby—recently ranked in the top seventy-five patent-law firms in the country by IP Today. Her team focuses on studying patents and other signals to predict future digital trends.

She has invested in and served on the boards of numerous technology start-up companies and was the first woman to serve as president of the Greater Cincinnati Venture Capital Association. Just a few of the clients she has served include: Microsoft, Nestlé, Procter & Gamble, Scripps Networks Interactive, Macy's, Duke Energy, and emerging technology companies. She is a certified Six Sigma black belt in process improvement, nationally accredited in public relations, and a regular contributor to *ClickZ* and *SEO Watch* on digital marketing, as well as national legal and technology publications about the future of the Internet, including *Executive Counsel, CIO Magazine, Bloomberg BusinessWeek, Inside Counsel, IP Frontline, E-Week,* the *National Law Journal,* and more.

She was appointed to and served on the Generic Names Supporting Organization (GNSO) Council of the Internet Corporation for Assigned Names and Numbers (ICANN) and was subsequently named chairwoman of the Independent Review of the GNSO. She has been recognized year after year as one of the top global three hundred intellectual-property strategists by *IAM* magazine, based in London. She is a graduate of the Direct Women Institute, an elite group of female executives being cultivated for public-company board service. She also completed the Stanford Law School Director's College Executive Education Program and is a member of the National Association of Corporate Directors.

This is her third book. Her previous books, *Domain Names Rewired* and *Brand Rewired,* published by Wiley, were widely recognized as forward-thinking, innovative approaches to brand development, protection by spanning silos within organizations, and recognizing future trends on the Internet. The books featured interviews with senior executives from Harley-Davidson, Scripps Networks, International Paper, General Mills, Yahoo!, Kraft Foods, Kimberly-Clark, Interbrand, J. Walter Thompson, Kodak, Procter & Gamble, Intel, Verizon, Time Warner, and Microsoft. It was also endorsed by senior executives at Microsoft, Procter & Gamble, Warner Bros. Entertainment, Richemont, and General Electric.

In addition to winning many awards for her global leadership, Jennifer is also widely recognized for her contributions to her local community. She is a member of the Tocqueville Society of the United Way and has chaired fundraising events for the American Red Cross, Leukemia & Lymphoma Society (named Woman of the Year) and the Film Commission in Cincinnati, Ohio.

If you'd like more information about Digital Mapping, auditing your company's digital strategy, or helping your company define the role of digital in the boardroom, you can find it at www.Boardroom.Solutions.

# BIBLIOGRAPHY BY CHAPTER

## CHAPTER 1

Ackerman, Jason. "Supermarkets." *Wall Street Journal*, 2015.

Ahmed, Ajaz and Stefan Olander. *Velocity: The Seven New Laws for a World Gone Digital*. Vermilion, 2012.

Alfredo K. "What Happens in an Internet Minute." October 20, 2015, http://www.hongkiat.com/blog/what-happens-in-an-internet-minute-infographic/.

Arbesman, Sam and Dane Stangler. *What Does Fortune 500 Turnover Mean?* The Ewin Marion Kauffman Foundation, 2012.

Atkinson, Robert D. and Stephen J. Ezell. *Innovation Economics: The Race for Global Advantage*. Yale University Press, 2012.

Banham, Russ. "Emerging Risk, Managing Threats in an Evolving Business World." *Wall Street Journal*, 2015.

Bensinger, Greg. "Rebuilding History's Biggest Dot-Com Bust." *Wall Street Journal*, 2015.

Berman, Laura. "The Joy of Sex, Updated." *Wall Street Journal*, 2015.

Carlson, Jennifer. "Guns." *Wall Street Journal*, 2015.

Coyne, Kevin, Patricia Clifford, and Renée Dye. "Breakthrough Thinking from Inside the Box." *Harvard Business Review*, 2007.

DeFrantz, Anita. "The Olympic Games in 2044." *Wall Street Journal*, 2015.

Diamond, Jared. *Collapse: How Societies Choose to Fail or Succeed*. Penguin, 2011.

Fadell, Tony. "All Around Us, Nothing but Net." *Wall Street Journal*, 2015.

Gertner, Jon. *The Idea Factory: Bell Labs and the Great Age of American Innovation.* Penguin, 2012.

Heppelmann, James and Michael Porter. "How Smart, Connected Products Are Transforming Competition." *Harvard Business Review*, 2014.

Huntsman, Jon. "Trade Gets More Important- and Complex." *Wall Street Journal*, 2015.

Jenkins, Holman W. Jr. "Google and the Self-Driving Delusion." *Wall Street Journal*, 2015.

Johnson, Steven. *How We Got to Now: Six Innovations That Made the Modern World.* Riverhead Books, 2014.

KnowledgeWorks Foundation. *2020 Forecast: Creating the Future of Learning.* KnowledgeWorks Foundation and Institute for the Future, 2008.

Kohsla, Sanjay and Mohanbir Sawhney. "Where to Look for Insight." *Harvard Business Review*, 2014.

Koller, Daphne. "Exit the Sage on the Stage." *Wall Street Journal*, 2015.

Levitt, Steven D. and Steven J. Dubner. *Super Freakonomics: Global Cooling, Patriotic Prostitutes and Why Suicide Bombers Should Buy Life Insurance.* HarperCollins, 2009.

McGonigal, Jane. "Is It a Game? Or is it Real?" *Wall Street Journal*, 2015.

Mosley, Walter. "What's Ahead for Winnie the Pooh." *Wall Street Journal*, 2015.

Nassauer, Sarah. "Stores Lead Shoppers by the Nose." *Wall Street Journal*, 2014.

ParisTech Review and Knowledge@Wharton. *2020 Foresight: Predictions for the next Decade*. ParisTech Review, 2011.

Pitt, Harvey. "Will Stock Exchanges Survive?" *Wall Street Journal*, 2015.

Reagan, Brad. "What do George Bailey, Jerry Maguire And Gordon Gekko Have in Common?" *Wall Street Journal*, 2013.

Richter, Felix. "E-Commerce in the United States." Statista.com. 2012.

Rigby, Darrell. "Digital-Physical Markups." *Harvard Business Review*, 2014.

Rocha, Euan. "BlackBerry CEO sees fewer new devices, focus on profitability." 2014, Reuters.com.

Schmidt, Eric and Jared Cohen. *The New Digital Age: Reshaping the Future of People, Nations and Business*. Alfred A. Knopf, 2013.

Silver, Nate. *The Signal and the Noise: Why So Many Predictions Fail—but Some Don't*. Penguin, 2012.

Sinek, Simon. *Start With Why: How Great Leaders Inspire Everyone to Take Action*. Penguin, 2011.

Stetka, Bret. "Go Ahead and Ask Others for Their DNA Results." *Wired*, 2014.

Thompson, Craig. "Get Ready for a Revolution in Cancer Care." *Wall Street Journal*, 2015.

Wong, Brian. "Farewell, Mass Marketing." *Wall Street Journal*, 2015.

## CHAPTER 2

Blanc, Dotty, Bart Boswinkel, Chris Disspain, and Demi Getschko. *Formation of the Country-Code Names Supporting Organization (ccNSO)*. 2004.

CNNMoney. "Verisign Buys Domain Firm." CNNMoney.com. 2000.

File, Thom. "Computer and Internet Use in the United States." https://www.census.gov/prod/2013pubs/p20-569.pdf.

Johnson, Bradley. "The Beginning of Everything." *Advertising Age*, 2013.

Silver, Elliot. "Vanity Fair Reveals Cost of Uber.com Domain Name." DomainInvesting.com. 2014.

Swisher, Kara. "Man and Uber Man." *Vanity Fair*, 2014.

"VeriSign.Inc.," Company-Histories.com. 2012.

## CHAPTER 3

"Letter from Chairman Rockefeller to Chairman White on SEC Guidance." April 9, 2013.

"Response Letter from Chairman White to Chairman Rockefeller on SEC Guidance." May 1, 2013.

Australian Government, Department of Defense, Cyber Security Operations Centre. "Strategies to Mitigate Targeted Cyber Intrusions." October 2012.

Basu, Eric. "Target CEO Fired- Can You Be Fired If Your Company is Hacked?" *Forbes*, 2014.

Blue Coat Systems. *Do Not Enter: Blue Coat Research Maps the Web's Shadiest Neighborhoods*. 2015.

Bowerman, Mary. "Minnesota dentist 'deeply' regrets 'taking' Cecil the lion." *USA Today*, 2015.

Cook, Tim. "On Encryption." *Wall Street Journal*, 2015.

Czarnecki, Gerald. "Cyber Threats Necessitate A New Governance Model." *NACD Directorship*, 2015.

Deiss, Ryan. "Customer Value Optimization: How to Build an Unstoppable Business." *Digital Marketer*, 2015.

Debouch, Jim. "Board Perspective on Risk." Protiviti.com. 2015.

Dwoskin, Elizabeth. "Data Privacy: Test Your Knowledge." *Wall Street Journal*, 2015.

———. "What is Encryption, Anyway?" *Wall Street Journal*, 2015.

Epstein, Adam. "Thinking Strategically About Cyber Risk." *NACD Directorship*, 2014.

Fenwick & West LLP. *Cybersecurity and the Board*. 2013.

———. *Reading Materials for Board Members on Cybersecurity Attacks*. June 24, 2013.

Gage, Deborah. "VCs Pour Money Into Cybersecurity Startups." *Wall Street Journal*, 2015.

Gibson, Dunn & Crutcher LLP. *Cyber-security and Data Privacy Outlook and Review: 2013*. April 16, 2013.

Harding, Luke. "How Edward Snowden went from loyal NSA contractor to whistleblower." *Guardian*, 2014.

Hilk, Jeff and Jeffry Powell. "Protecting Your Board Books." *National Association of Corporate Directors*ship September, 2014.

Huang, Daniel. "United They Stand." *Wall Street Journal*, 2015.

Keller, Punam. "I Should Worry. But I Don't." *Wall Street Journal*, 2015.

Kokalitcheva, Kia. "Fake Bloomberg news report drives Twitter Stock up 8%." *Fortune*, 2015.

Lee, Edmund. "AP Twitter Account Hacked in Market-Moving Attack." *Bloomberg Business Week*, 2013.

Marchand, Ashley. "Environmental and Competitive Disruptors Likely to Transform Board Agendas." *National Association of Corporate Directorship*, September, 2014.

Miller, Greg. "'The Snowden Files: The Inside Story of the World's Most Wanted Man', by Luke Harding." *Washington Post*, 2014.

National Association of Corporate Directors. *Cyber-Risk Oversight: Director's Handbook Series.* 2014.

———. *Questions for the Board to Ask Management about Cybersecurity.* 2015.

———. *Report for the 2015 NACD Blue Ribbon Commission: The Board and Long-Term Value Creation.* 2015.

Neustar, Inc. *April 2015 Neustar DDOS Attacks & Protection Report: North America.* 2015.

"New Cybersecurity Governance Study Shows Dramatic Increase in Boards Addressing Cyber Risks." CNN.com. 2015.

Paletta, Damian. "Cyberwar Ignites New Arms Race." *Wall Street Journal*, 2015.

PC Magazine Encyclopedia. "Deep Web Definition."

PricewaterhouseCoopers White Paper Series. "Cybersecurity is front and center." PwC, 2015.

———. "Director confidence about cybersecurity." PwC, 2015.

———. "IT strategy and IT risk mitigation." PwC, 2015.

———. "Time spent on IT oversight." PwC, 2015.

———. *Turnaround and transformation in cybersecurity: Key findings from The Global State of Information Security Survey 2015* pwc.com/gsiss.

———. "Where do directors want to spend more time?" PwC, 2015.

———. "Who oversees IT risks?" PwC, 2015.

PricewaterhouseCoopers Center for Board Governance. *Directors and IT: What Works Best: A user-friendly board Guide for Information Technology Oversight*, abridged ed. 2012.

Samuel, Alexandra. "The Weakest Security Link: Your Children." *Wall Street Journal*, 2015.

Securities and Exchange Commission, Division of Corporation Finance. *CF Disclosure Guidance: Topic No. 2 Cybersecurity*. October 13 2011. Smith, Gerry. "New York Post Confirms Twitter Accounts Were Hacked." *Bloomberg Business*, 2015.

Swarts, Angela. "CEO heads may roll for security breaches in wake of Sony boss' exit, experts say." *Silicon Valley Business Journal*, 2015.

Symantec Corporation. *White Paper: Protecting Against Web Application Threats Using SSL.* 2013.

Tapestry Networks. *Cybersecurity and the Board, Audit Committee Leadership Network in North America.* November 7, 2012.

Vijayan, Jaikumar. "Target breach happened because of a basic network segmentation error." *Computerworld*, 2014.

Wallace, Gregory. "HVAC vendor eyed as entry point for Target breach." CNN.com., 2014.

Yadron, Danny. "Ashley Madison's Stolen Data Is Posted." *Wall Street Journal*, 2015.

———. "The Man Who Finds the Security Holes." *Wall Street Journal*, 2015.

———. "What Companies Should Be Doing to Protect Their Computer Systems- but Aren't." *Wall Street Journal*, 2015.

## CHAPTER 4

"Black Hat Vs White Hat." Smart Solutions, 2014.

"Coca-Cola's Million Dollar Hug." Brandchannel.com. 2012.

"How Will New gTLDS Affect Search Engine Optimisation?" Domainmonster.com. 2013.

"Internet Users in the World Distributed by World Regions- 2015 Q2." *Internet World Stats.* Minimarts Marketing Group, 2015.

"Metadata- Discoverability and Liability." *WriterinLaw.com.* 2013.

"Total Number of Websites." Netcraft and Internet Live Stats.

Amerland, David. *Google Semantic Search: Search Engine Optimization (SEO) Techniques That Get Your Company More Traffic, Increase Brand Impact, and Amplify Your Online Presence.* Pearson Education, 2014.

Banjo, Shelly and Sara Germano. "The End of the Impulse Shopper." *Wall Street Journal*, 2014.

Cocek, Aleksandar. "The Guide to Creating and Optimizing Metadata for SEO." 2014, http://www.cyberalert.com/blog/index.php/the-guide-to-creating-and-optimizing-metadata-for-seo/.

Cutts, Matt. "Explaining algorithm updates and data refreshes." Google Blog, 2006.

―――. "Gadgets, Google, and SEO." 2009.

―――. "Gadgets, Google, and SEO." 2013.

Dean, Brian. "Google's 200 Ranking Factors: The Complete List." 2014, http://backlinko.com/google-ranking-factors.

Ehrlich, Serena. "SEO Best Practices: The Impact of Social Media on Search Engine Optimization." 2014, https://www.bulldogreporter.com/seo-best-practices-the-impact-of-social-media-on-search-engine-opti/.

Eisenberg, Jeremy. "Is Metadata Still Important Today?" 2014, http://3pcreativegroup.com/is-metadata-still-important/.

Elran, Asher. "What Google 'Hummingbird' Means for Your SEO Strategy." 2013, Entrepreneur.com.

Enge, Eric. "5 Keys to Improving Search Rankings with Duane Forrester of Bing." 2014, https://www.stonetemple.com/duane-forresters-5-keys-to-improving-search-rankings/.

Fleischner, Michael H. *SEO Made Simple: Strategies for Dominating the World's Largest Search Engine*. Michael H. Fleischner, 2013.

Garner, Rob. *Search & Social: The Definitive Guide to Real-Time Content Marketing*. John Wiley & Sons, 2013.

Google Inc. "Our History in depth." 2014.

Jones, James and Craig Landes. *A+ Exam Cram 2*. Que Certification, 2003.

Kolowich, Lindsay. "The Evolution of SEO [Infographic]." 2014, https://blog.hubspot.com/marketing/evolution-of-seo.

McCarthy, Kieren. "How to hit the top of Google's rankings: 'Use a new dot-thing gTLD.'" *The Register*, 2014.

Moz.com. "Google Algorithm Change History." 2015, https://moz.com/google-algorithm-change.

Ngak, Chenda. "As Google Fiber expands to Olathe, Kan., millions of Americans still offline." 2013, http://www.cbsnews.com/news/as-google-fiber-expands-to-olathe-kan-millions-of-americans-still-offline/.

Peters, J. "Google Updates: A History of SEO from 2000–2010." 2010, http://www.bruceclay.com/blog/google-updates-a-history-of-seo-from-2000-2010/

Piombino, Kristin. "Infographic: Factors that affect your SEO ranking." 2013, http://www.ragan.com/Main/Articles/Infographic_Factors_that_affect_your_SEO_ranking_47317.aspx.

Schmitz, Tom. "2014 SEO Playbook: Google Hummingbird, Content & Authority." 2013, http://searchengineland.com/2014-seo-playbook-part-1-hummingbird-175860.

Shebel, Melanie. "What Meta Tags Are & How to Optimize Metadata for SEO." 2014, http://hubpages.com/business/Meta-Data-for-SEO.

Williams, Andy. *SEO 2014 & Beyond: Search Engine Optimization Will Never be the Same Again!* CreateSpace, 2013.

## CHAPTER 5

"The 13 Scariest Social Media Fails by Brands this Year." 2014, http://www.mdgadvertising.com/blog/the-13-scariest-social-media-fails-by-brands-this-year/.

Albergotti, Reed. "Facebook Warns of Higher Costs." *Wall Street Journal*, 2014.

Albergotti, Reed and Alistair Barr. "Facebook is Set for a Digital-Ad Duel." *Wall Street Journal*, 2014.

Carlson, Nicholas. "At Last—The Full Story of How Facebook was Founded." *Business Insider.com*, 2010.

Gaille, Brandon. "42 Do's and Don'ts of Social Media Marketing." 2015,

Guimarães, Thiago. "Revealed: A Breakdown of the Demographics for Each of the Different Social Networks." *Business Insider*, 2015.

Halligan, Brian & Shah, Dharmesh. *Inbound Marketing: Attract, Engage, and Delight Customers Online*. John Wiley & Sons, 2014.

McCarty, Brad. "The History of the Smartphone." *TNWNEWS*, 2011.

Pozin, Ilya. "20 Companies You Should Be Following on Social Media." *Forbes*, 2014.

Regan, Kadie. "10 Amazing Social Media Growth Stats from 2015." *Social Media Today*, 2015.

Wagstaff, Ketih. "Ellen's Oscar Selfie—Worth $1 Billion?" NBC News, 2014.

## CHAPTER 6

"With Big Data Comes Big Responsibility: An Interview with Alex 'Sandy' Pentland." *Harvard Business Review*, 2014.

Balasubramanian, Manikandan and Pramath Malik. "In search of the next patent war." *Intellectual Asset Management Magazine*, 2015.

Bhuiyan, Johana and Charlie Warzel. "'God View': Uber Investigates Its Top New York Executive For Privacy Violations." BuzzFeed.com., 2014.

Chapin, Lyman, Scott Eldridge, and Karen Rose. "The Internet of Things: An Overview." TheInternetSociety.org.

Dredge, Stuart. "91% of top brands have apps, but how many of them are any good?" *The Guardian*, 2011.

Heppelmann, James and Michael Porter. "How Smart, Connected Products are Transforming Competition." *Harvard Business Review*, 2014.

Hirschauge, Orr and Deepa Seetharaman. "Facebook Looks to Bring Virtual Reality to Mobile Devices." *Wall Street Journal*, 2015.

Laurie, Ron. "Constructing a holistic corporate patent monetization strategy." *Intellectual Asset Management Magazine*, 2015.

Matte, Daniel and Kevin McCullagh. "Will Smartwatches Be a Hit?" *Wall Street Journal*, 2015.

Mui, Chunka and Paul B. Carroll. *The New Killer Apps: How Large Companies can Out-Innovate Start-Ups*. Cornerloft Press, 2013.

Oliver, Erik and Kent Richardson. "The strategic counter-assertion model for patent portfolio RoI." *Intellectual Asset Management Magazine*, 2015.

Tepper, Nona. "Nearly two-thirds of B2B companies have mobile web sites and apps." *Internet Retailer*, 2015.

Topol, Eric. "Your Smartphone Will See You Now." *Wall Street Journal*, 2015.

Vonck, Richard. "Connecting with Our Connected World." *The Futurist*. World Future Society, 2013.

"Scenario: Life with the Internet of Everything." *The Futurist*. World Future Society, 2013.

## CHAPTER 7
"Google Seeks Richer Role With Own Content." *Wall Street Journal*, 2014.

"Sharma, Amol and Shalini Ramachandran. "HBO Explores the 'How' of Streaming Option." *Wall Street Journal*, 2014.

Cook, Tim. "Tim Cook: TV, Cars, Watches and More." *Wall Street Journal*, 2015.

Fritz, Ben. "Home-Entertainment Sales Resume Slide; VOD Down." *Wall Street Journal*, 2015.

Goldman, Jake and Ben Ilfeld. "iOS 9 Content Blockers: Impact Analysis and Mitigating Strategies." 10up.com. 2015.

Gottfried, Miriam. "How Cable Companies Can Capture the Mobile Internet." *Wall Street Journal*, 2015.

Morrison, Maureen. "The CMO's Guide to Messaging Apps." *Advertising Age*, 2015.

Morrison, Maureen and Tim Peterson. "The War on Advertising." *Advertising Age*, 2015.

Oh, Soo Jin. "Buyer Behavior Trends Driving the Digital Shift Toward Mobile." *Marketing Land, June 18,* 2015, marketingland.com.

Peterson, Tim. "Entertainment's engineers: How video is being reprogrammed at YouTube." *Advertising Age*, 2015.

Poggi, Jeanine. "Sling TV CMO courts cord cutters, is careful not to undercut Dish TV." *Advertising Age*, 2015.

Wakabayashi, Daisuke. "E-BOOK." *Wall Street Journal*, 2015.

# CHAPTER 8

"What are Cookies?" Slightlyinteresting.com, 2015.

Accenture. *Marketing Mission-Critical*. 2012.

Berman, Dennis and Jerry Wolfe. "Big Data's Promise, Peril." *Wall Street Journal*, 2015.

Brown, Brad et al. *Big data: The next frontier for innovation, competition and productivity*. McKinsey & Company, 2011.

Clifton, Brian. "Successful Analytics: Gain Business Insights by Managing Google Analytics." Advanced Web Metrics, 2015.

CMO C-Suite Studies. "From Stretched to Strengthened: Insights from the Global Chief Marketing Officer Study." IBM Corporation, 2011.

Columbus, Louis. "The Best Big Data and Business Analytics Companies to Work for In 2015." *Forbes*, 2015.

Dwoskin, Elizabeth and Deepa Seetharaman. "Facebook Restricts Access to Its Data Trove." *Wall Street Journal*, 2015.

Kaplan, Phillip J. *F'd Companies: Spectacular Dot-Com Flameouts*. Simon & Schuster, 2002.

Kapner, Suzanne. "Data Pushes Aside Chief Merchants." *Wall Street Journal*, 2015.

Kurzweil, Ray. "The New, Improved You." *Wall Street Journal*, 2014.

Lloyd, Richard. "The Rise of the Google Gorilla." *Intellectual Asset Management Magazine*, 2015.

Marshall, Jack. "Apple Propels Cottage Industry of Ad Blockers." *Wall Street Journal*, 2015.

Seetharaman, Deepa. "Oculus Adds Movies and TV." *Wall Street Journal*, 2015.

## CHAPTER 9

Bill Gates Biography, The Biography.com.

Cloyd, Mary Ann. "Taking a Fresh Look at Board Composition." *PricewaterhouseCoopers LLP*. 2013.

Hubbard, Douglas W. *How to Measure Anything: Finding the Value of Intangibles in Business*. John Wiley & Sons, 2007.

PricewaterhouseCoopers. "Governing for the long term: Looking down the road with an eye on the rear –view mirror." PwC. 2015.

Shai Bernstein Stanford Graduate School of Business. "Does Going Public Affect Innovation?" Research Paper No. 212, December 2012.

Solis, Brian. *What's the Future of Business? Changing the Way Businesses Create Experiences.* John Wiley & Sons, 2013.

I have referred to various patents throughout the book, all of which are a matter of public record in the United States. You can search patents for free through patents.google.com or on the upsto.gov websites. If you have questions about how to research or use patents, please contact Jwolfe@dotbrand360.agency.

www.ingramcontent.com/pod-product-compliance
Lightning Source LLC
Chambersburg PA
CBHW030927180526
45163CB00002B/486